beautiful BRIDAL ACCESSORIES *you can make*

Jacquelynne Johnson

beautiful BRIDAL ACCESSORIES *you can make*

Jacquelynne Johnson

BETTERWAY BOOKS

CINCINNATI, OHIO

www.artistsnetwork.com

06 05 04 03 02   5 4 3 2 1
Library of Congress Cataloging-in-Publication Data
Johnson, Jacquelynne.
Beautiful bridal accessories you can make / by Jacquelynne Johnson.
   p.cm.
Includes bibliographical references and index.
ISBN 1-55870-624-0 (pbk. : alk. paper)
1. Wedding costume. 2. Dress accessories. 3. Handicraft. I. Title.
TT633 .J64 2002
745.594'1--dc21

                        2002071204

EDITORS: Tricia Waddell, Karen Roberts and Jolie Lamping Roth
DESIGNER: Andrea Short
LAYOUT ARTIST: Cheryl VanDeMotter
PRODUCTION COORDINATOR: Sara Dumford
PHOTOGRAPHERS: Tim Grondin and Al Parrish
STYLIST: Jan Nickum

DEDICATION

I dedicate this book to three: Most of all to The Lord, for giving me the courage to create this book. I am also grateful to Tracey Kokumo, a kindred spirit and so much more. And I am especially thankful for my husband, Raymond, who never ceased to believe in and pray for the success of this project.

ACKNOWLEDGMENTS

Thanks to Tricia Waddell, Karen Roberts, Jolie Lamping Roth, Greg Albert, Tim Grondin, Andrea Short, Jennifer Johnson and Julia Groh for their input and relentless striving for perfection. Special thanks to my friends Donna Bowden, Maxine Dillard, Roberta Mitchell, Cheire Mullane and Melissa Smith. And I owe enormous gratitude to Jessie McGee, Rebecca Broadnax, Judith Moore and Seka Soun.

INTRODUCTION

HAVE YOU EVER WONDERED WHAT IT WOULD BE LIKE TO MAKE YOUR OWN WEDDING ACCESSORIES? BEAUTIFUL BRIDAL ACCESSORIES YOU CAN MAKE ALLOWS EVERY CRAFTER TO RE-CREATE THESE LOVELY BRIDAL ACCESSORIES BEAUTIFULLY WITH A BIT OF PATIENCE. WHETHER YOU ARE A SEWING BEGINNER OR AN EXPERIENCED SEAMSTRESS, THIS BOOK HAS BEEN CREATED WITH YOU IN MIND. BEAUTIFUL BRIDAL ACCESSORIES YOU CAN MAKE SEEKS TO REVEAL THE INNER CREATIVITY AND CAPABILITY THAT EXISTS IN EVERY READER, NO MATTER THE LEVEL OF EXPERTISE. NOT ONLY CAN THE READER BE CREATIVE, BUT THE CREATION CAN BE EXQUISITE AND ELEGANT.

This book is designed to encourage every reader to experience the joys of sewing without frustration or difficulty. The craft projects provide detailed step-by-step instruction with illustrations to guide you through the process. For your convenience, there are lists of materials, so you can easily shop for all of the items you need before beginning the projects. In addition, the resource section details a list of Internet resources, should you desire a greater variety of designs than those available in your area. Finally, the techniques are simple and can be learned in a short amount of time.

Using your creativity, energy and talent can produce projects that will give you years of enjoyment. But like all crafts or art, it will take patience and some practice. I have learned the hard way that there is no such thing as a "two-minute project." The finished piece will demonstrate that you have invested time, patience and creativity. Remember, creating beautiful projects takes time, but creating elegant projects takes time and patience. In other words, calmness, perseverance and determination will make the undertaking of any creative project a successful and happy one.

Don't worry if sometimes the creativity in you wants to rest; let your creative mind have some time off. Believe it or not, sometimes I don't feel like working on a project. It's not that I don't have anything to do; I'm just not in the mood. Know this can happen to all crafters. If you do not feel like working on your project, don't. Never push yourself. Just let things come. It will be better to take your time.

It is my hope that you will find the designs easy-to-follow so your sewing experience is rewarding and fun. I encourage all fellow "glue gun" enthusiasts to join me as we create something elegant together in celebration of the wedding tradition. May every thread, fabric, adornment and spot of glue pave the way to something beautiful for you and yours.

GOD BLESS! *Jackie*

ICON KEY

project requires a sewing machine

PROJECT RATINGS

= easy

= intermediate

= advanced

HELPFUL HINTS

•••

1 Give yourself plenty of time for any sewing project that goes beyond what you've done before.

2 Good tools are essential. Not only will they save you time, they will help you produce superior results. Good scissors and good thread are a must.

3 Test all the fabrics you are using in a project. Can they withstand moisture? Can you iron them safely? Should they be prewashed? Can they be dry-cleaned or washed by hand? Ask the salesperson at the fabric store if you are not sure about how to care for your chosen fabrics.

4 Always buy more fabric than you need in case you make a mistake or want to make more than one of the same project.

Basic Tools and Supplies

Most of the projects in this book require basic crafting skills, tools and supplies. If you know how to use a glue gun, you can easily complete half the projects in this book. The other half of the projects require basic sewing supplies for handstitching or a sewing machine. Look for the **sewing machine symbol** for projects that require the use of a sewing machine for completion. To complete the simple sewing projects in this book, you will need the following tools:

FABRIC SHEARS • Make sure you have a good, sharp pair of fabric shears for cutting ribbon, fabric and lace. Never use fabric shears on wired ribbon or paper because it will dull the blade. Keep a separate pair of craft scissors for non-fabric items.

EMBROIDERY SCISSORS • These small scissors are great for intricate projects that require delicate cutting in small spaces.

RULER AND TAPE MEASURE • Make sure your measuring tools show both inches and centimeters.

NEEDLES • The best hand-sewing needles for these projects are size 9 or 10 millimeters. For beading projects, use an extra-fine beading needle.

THREAD • All the projects in this book call for 40 wt. thread. This thread is strong enough for hand sewing, and it won't kink or break easily like lightweight threads.

Basic Stitching

Here is a quick reference guide to the basic stitches used throughout this book.

BACKSTITCH • Make a short stitch. Insert the needle at the beginning of this stitch and bring it out a stitch ahead. The result should resemble machine-stitching and be neat and regular.

RUNNING STITCH • This is the simplest of all stitches. It is created by pulling the needle up through the fabric and pushing it down through the fabric, spacing the entry and departure point to the desired length.

SLIP STITCH • Pick up a thread or two of the fabric. Then run the needle inside the folded edge about ¼" (6mm) and again pick up a thread or two.

BASTING • Basting basically means to use a large running stitch, about 1" (3cm) long.

Choosing Fabrics

Once you have the right sewing and crafting tools for a project, you will need to choose fabrics and embellishments. Bridal fabrics are luxurious, glamorous and delicate. Depending on your sewing experience, they can often be intimidating to work with, too. On the opposite page, you will find a guide to the most common bridal fabrics and laces. Depending on the weight of the fabric, you can substitute almost any of these fabrics for the specific ones used in the step-by-step projects. Use the same fabric or lace in your dress to make complementary accessories for you and your wedding party.

There are a wide variety of decorative ribbons available in craft and fabric stores. Use the Decorative Ribbon Guide to choose just the right finishing touch to accent a project, from a bridal headband to a keepsake ring pillow.

Whether you are choosing fabrics or embellishments for your projects, take your cue from the style of your wedding, the season, your wedding colors and flowers, your wedding attire, and overall wedding decor. But more importantly, use your imagination and go with what fits your personal style.

Bridal Fabric Guide
•••

BATISTE	*Fine, plain-woven fabric made from various fibers*
BROCADE	*Heavy fabric woven with a rich, raised design*
CHARMEUSE	*Satin-finished silk fabric*
CHIFFON	*Sheer silk or rayon fabric, often layered over heavier, stiffer and shinier fabrics*
CREPE	*Light, soft, thin fabric of silk, cotton or wool with a crinkled surface*
CREPE DE CHINE	*Silk crepe with a soft drape*
EYELET	*Cotton fabric with small holes edged with embroidered stitches*
FAILLE	*Slightly ribbed, woven fabric of silk, cotton or rayon*
GEORGETTE	*Sheer, strong silk or silky clothing fabric with a dull crepe surface*
MOIRÉ	*Silk or rayon, finished so as to have a wavy or rippled surface pattern*
ORGANZA	*Sheer, stiff fabric of silk or synthetic material*
SATIN	*Smooth fabric made of silk or rayon*
SHANTUNG	*Heavy fabric with a rough, nubby surface, made of spun wild silk*
TAFFETA	*Crisp, smooth, plain woven fabric with a slight sheen*
TULLE	*Fine net of silk, rayon or nylon*
VELVET	*Soft fabric made of silk, rayon or nylon with a smooth dense pile and plain underside*

Lace Glossary
•••

ALENÇON	*Net background with a solid design and needlepoint lace*
BRUSSELS	*Delicate lace with subtle patterns*
CHANTILLY	*Floral or scroll designs on a mesh-like pattern*
CLUNY	*An open design made with fine linen thread*
FRENCH	*Machine-made lace fabrics made to look like handmade French lace*
GUIPURE	*Heavy needlepoint lace with large patterns*
RENAISSANCE	*Heavy, flat lace of various stitches joined with tape*
SCHIFFLI	*Machine-made delicate floral embroidery*
SPANISH	*Flat design of roses on a mesh background*
VENISE	*Needlepoint lace of foliage or geometric designs*

Decorative Ribbon Guide
•••

GROSGRAIN	*Woven ribbon with a crosswise pattern*
JACQUARD	*Ribbon with an intricately woven pattern, often with a tapestry look*
METALLIC	*Ribbon made with shiny or iridescent metal fibers for a sparkled look*
ORGANDY	*Sheer and often iridescent ribbon made of contrasting colored yarns*
SATIN	*Available in single or double-faced; sometimes has a feather or picot edge*
SHEER	*Plain, print or striped almost transparent ribbon, often with a thick thread woven along the edge*
TAFFETA	*Crisp, smooth plain-woven ribbon with a slight sheen*
TWILL	*Ribbon with diagonal parallel lines*
WIRE EDGE CRAFT RIBBON	*Ribbon with soft wire woven into the edge to help it hold its shape*

EMBELLISHMENTS

EASY-TO-FIND EMBELLISHMENTS

•••

Turn ordinary items into something unique with easy-to-find materials. Here are a few of the most common embellishments; use your imagination to find the items that reflect your personality and interest. The possibilities are endless.

- Antique heirlooms
- Appliqués
- Beads
- Charms
- Cording
- Fabric trimmings
- Gemstones
- Lace
- Pearls
- Pressed flowers
- Ribbons
- Rosettes
- Sequins
- Silk & dried flowers
- Tassels
- Tulle

Personalizing Your Wedding

The wedding ceremony is an expression of love and a time to share your hopes and dreams for the future with your family and friends. It is a beginning, one that you will want to cherish.

Every bride wants her wedding to be unique, and there are some easy, creative, inexpensive ways to express your individual style to add beauty, detail and meaning to ordinary wedding accessories. From headpieces to shoes, embellishments change the ordinary into extraordinary. Start with the basics—plain shoes or toasting flutes—and add your special touch using flowers, beads, ribbons, lace, pearls or charms, anything that may hold special meaning to you or your fiancé.

Tying the Knots

Unmatched accessories are loose ends you don't want left untied, so use embellishing to coordinate your colors and wedding theme in all areas, from the ceremony to the reception.

•••

Your wedding.
Your special touch.
Your unique style.

•••

(ABOVE) **BRIDAL HANDBAG** • *Pearls, sequins and beads make this elegant handbag sparkle. Just big enough to carry a few wedding day necessities, this exquisite bag is the perfect accessory.*

(ABOVE) **CAKE KNIFE AND SERVER** • *Ribbons, beads and pearls transform a plain cake knife and server into a beautiful cake-cutting showpiece. Embellish your cake knife and server set to complement your wedding cake and toasting flutes.*

(LEFT) **WEDDING GLOVES** • *Transform plain gloves into a stylish accessory by adding a little ribbon and lace. Beautiful decorative ribbons such as this pearl trimmed organza ribbon can add just the right finishing touch to any bridal accessory.*

TRANSFORM THE ORDINARY INTO EXTRAORDINARY

Let your uniqueness shine through with handcrafted wedding accessories. Here are a few common items that are easy to jazz up using your special touch. Use this list as a springboard to spark your creativity. Make your special day more special—Embellish!

- Cake knife and server
- Gloves
- Guest book
- Hair accessories
- Hosiery
- Photo albums
- Ring bearer pillow
- Shoes
- Toasting Flutes
- Unity candle

remember...

Too much embellishment may be distracting. Make sure your embellishments complement the objects, not overpower them. Sometimes a light touch is all that is needed.

SECTION 1

WEARABLE
ACCESSORIES

THE PERFECT DRESS DESERVES PERFECT ACCESSORIES. USE THE IDEAS IN THIS

SECTION TO DESIGN AND CREATE THE ACCESSORIES YOU'VE ALWAYS WANTED. FROM

HEAD TO TOE, YOU CAN ADD YOUR SPECIAL TOUCH TO YOUR WEDDING ENSEMBLE

AND ACHIEVE THE PERFECT LOOK. AND REMEMBER, BEAUTIFUL ACCESSORIES ARE

NOT ONLY FOR THE BRIDE. CREATE ACCESSORIES ESPECIALLY FOR YOUR FLOWER GIRL

OR AS A SPECIAL GIFT FOR EVERYONE IN THE BRIDAL PARTY. USE RIBBONS, PEARLS,

FLOWERS, OR ANY OTHER MATERIALS THAT COORDINATE WITH YOUR WEDDING

ENSEMBLE, AND LET YOUR CREATIVITY TAKE OVER.

BRIDAL WRAP · BRIDAL HANDBAG · BRIDAL HEADPIECE & VEIL · FLOWER GIRL HEADBAND · PEARL BARRETTE

BRIDAL WRAP

Look stunning by wrapping yourself in yards of frothy organza and delicate lace. A luxurious bridal wrap is the perfect complement to any romantic strapless, sleeveless or thin-strapped gown. For sheer beauty, drape the wrap around your shoulders or gather it gracefully with an elegant brooch. Choose from a range of luxurious fabrics to design your wrap, from sheer chiffon, georgette and organza to sensuous silk shantung, crepe de chine and velvet— any fabric that drapes well and feels deliriously dramatic on your skin will do. Leave it elegantly simple or trim with lace, beads, pearls or whatever accents your dress. Keep the wrap beautifully understated with an ornate dress or add more embellishments to the wrap if you are wearing a simple, clean-lined dress.

materials:

- 33" x 72" (84cm x 2m) organza
- 1 yd. (1m) guipure lace
- flat–back rhinestones
- fabric glue
- white 40 wt. thread
- hand-sewing needle

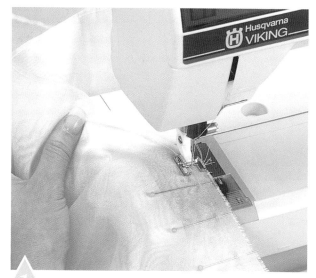

1 Sew the Organza

With the right sides of the organza together, fold it in half lengthwise and pin. Stitch a ¼" (6mm) seam allowance, leaving a 6" (15cm) opening on the long side for turning it inside out, as shown in the diagram.

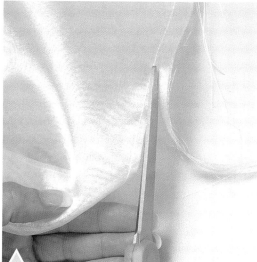

2 Trim the Seam

Use scissors to trim the excess organza close to the seam allowance along the three completely stitched sides of the wrap. Turn the organza right side out and press it with a warm iron. Slip stitch the 6" (15cm) opening close by hand.

```
fold line




• ←  stop here  → •
```

3 Hand Sew the Lace

Pin the guipure lace to each end of the sheer wrap and cut away the excess. Following the shape of the motifs, hand stitch the lace in place.

4 Glue the Rhinestones

Place a rhinestone on your index finger with the flat side facing upwards. Place a dab of fabric glue on the flat side. Decorate the lace motif with rhinestones according to your preference.

• keepsake handkerchief

Now you can wipe away your

wedding day tears of joy in style.

Create a keepsake handkerchief

with the same fabric and appliqué

trim as the wrap. Cut your fabric

to 9" x 11" (23cm x 28cm) and

turn under the raw edges ¼"

(6mm) on all sides. Press and turn

pressed edge again. Hand stitch

the lace on all sides. This elegant

handkerchief makes a cherished

gift for your bridesmaids or

mother. Or make it out of cotton

or satin and offer it as a romantic

gift to your groom on your

wedding day.

it's a wrap!

The great thing about this wrap is you can customize it to fit your wedding style in a million ways. Instead of lace, add satin ribbon on the short ends or stitch small ribbon roses or trim along the edge. If you decide against wearing a veil, make a stunning wrap out of yards of tulle. Simply tie the ends of the tulle with a satin bow and float down the aisle in high style.

BRIDAL HANDBAG

A small, chic handbag can add a special touch to any wedding ensemble. It should be just big enough for carrying a lipstick and compact for quick touch-ups during the reception. For the bride, the focal point is you and your gown, so your bridal handbag should be understated, elegant and sophisticated. Choose a fabric that matches your dress for the perfect accessory. This handbag is made of delicately woven ivory damask, lined with satin and closes with a snap. Silver bugle beads, sequins and pearls are tenderly hand-strung and stitched in place for a look of timeless elegance.

materials:

- ½ yd. (46cm) damask fabric
- ½ yd. (46cm) lining fabric
- ½ yd. (46cm) fusible interfacing
- 4mm pearls
- 5mm sequins
- 4mm drop pearls
- 2mm silver bugle beads
- 3mm silver-lined rochaille
- #1 sew-on snap
- 2½" x 4½" (6cm x 11cm) cardboard
- white 40 wt. thread
- hand-sewing needle
- extra-fine beading needle

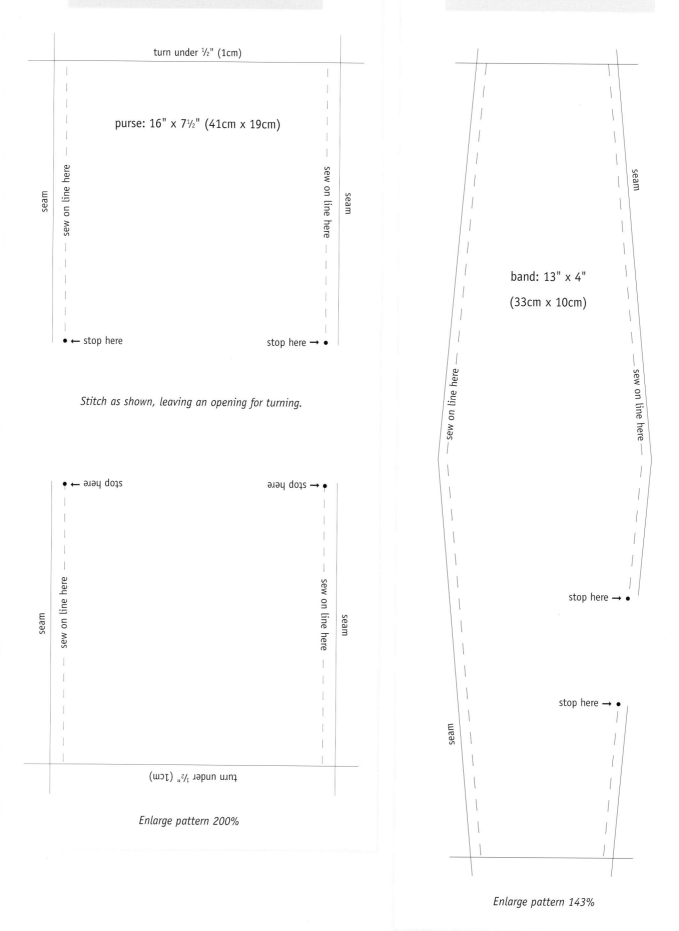

PATTERN FOR PURSE

turn under ½" (1cm)

purse: 16" x 7½" (41cm x 19cm)

seam

sew on line here

seam

sew on line here

• ← stop here

stop here → •

Stitch as shown, leaving an opening for turning.

• ← stop here

stop here → •

seam

sew on line here

seam

sew on line here

turn under ½" (1cm)

Enlarge pattern 200%

PATTERN FOR STRAP

band: 13" x 4"

(33cm x 10cm)

seam

sew on line here

seam

sew on line here

stop here → •

seam

stop here → •

Enlarge pattern 143%

1 Cut Out the Pattern

With the fabric face down, lay the fusible interfacing on top and fuse it to the fabric with a warm iron. Do not use the fusible interfacing on the lining, only on the purse fabric. Pin the purse and strap patterns to the fabric and cut the fabric according to the patterns. Transfer the pattern marks to the wrong side of the fabric. Repeat this step for the lining fabric but without the fusible interfacing.

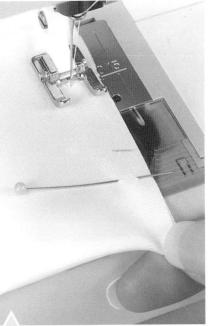

2 Sew the Side Seam

Fold the fabric with the fusible interfacing so that the right sides of the fabric are together, and pin in place. Stitch the raw edges on both of the side seams to the stop line only. Repeat this step with the lining fabric. Turn both pieces inside out and press.

3 Form the Bottom of the Handbag

Open the handbag fabric at the bottom and pull it apart to form the letter "T." Pin it in place.

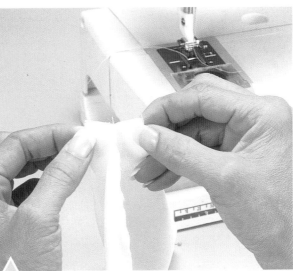

4 Sew the "T"

Stitch both sides of the "T" from the outside edge to the center seam line. Repeat this step with the lining fabric.

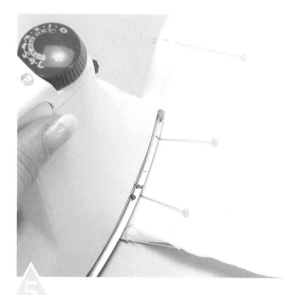

5 Press the Edge

Turn down the raw edge at the top of the handbag ½" (1cm). Pin it in place and press. Repeat this step with the lining fabric but do not sew it yet; put aside for now.

6 Sew the Handbag Strap

With the right sides together, pin the strap lining to the strap fabric and stitch a ¼" (6mm) seam allowance on both sides, leaving a 3" (8cm) opening for turning. Do not sew the ends of the strap. Trim a scant ⅛" (3mm) of excess fabric from the seam allowance. Turn the strap right side out and press. Slip stitch the opening together.

EMERGENCY WEDDING DAY KIT

◆

Always expect the unexpected. While your handbag may only carry your lipstick, a compact and some tissues, don't forget to keep a small stash of the following emergency items in your dressing room on your wedding day—just in case.

- aspirin
- breath mints
- bottled water
- snacks
- extra makeup
- hand mirror
- hair spray
- hand lotion
- cotton swabs
- sanitary napkins
- clear nail polish
- nail file
- nail glue

- safety pins
- baby powder
- stapler
- sewing kit
- extra pairs of hosiery
- straws (to avoid messing up your lipstick)
- white chalk (to cover up lipstick stains on a wedding dress)
- masking tape (quick repair for hems)

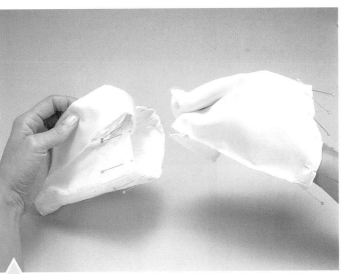

Insert the Cardboard

Trace the bottom of the handbag onto the cardboard. Cut the cardboard to fit inside the bottom of the handbag and insert.

Insert the Lining

With one end free, pin the raw edge of the strap down ½" (1cm) and to the center of the fold line. Insert the lining into the handbag. Pin the lining in place around the edge, leaving an opening for the other end of strap to be sewn in later.

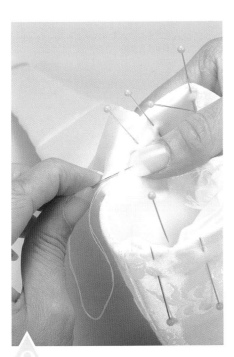

Stitch the Lining to the Handbag

On the inside of the handbag, slip stitch the lining to the handbag. Insert the other end of the strap in place and continue to slip stitch the lining to the handbag. Cut and tie off the thread to secure.

on your wedding day...

During the ceremony, ask someone who is not a part of your wedding party to hold your bridal handbag for you, then ask a bridesmaid to make sure it makes it to your seat at the reception.

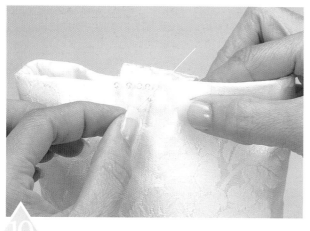

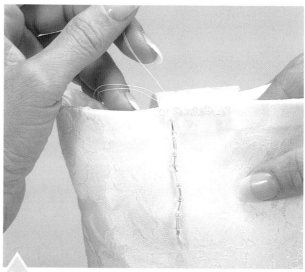

10 Start the Beading Pattern

For row 7, thread an extra-fine beading needle and knot the end of the thread. Each strand in row 7 will have a sequin and pearl only. Begin at one side of the strap and insert the needle into the top fabric. Bring the needle up and out, then add one clear sequin and one 4mm pearl. Go back through the clear sequin and the fabric, giving the thread a tug. Make a tiny backstitch and clip the thread to 3" (8cm). Hand tie the thread with three knots and clip the excess thread. Repeat this step six more times to complete row 7 (the top row) of beading.

·tip·

Rub beeswax or candle wax on the thread to keep it from tangling.

11 Complete the Beading Pattern

Each row has the same number of strands as the row number. For example, row 6 has six beading strands. To begin each strand in row 6, thread a 4mm pearl, 2mm silver bugle bead, 3mm silver-lined rochaille, and 2mm silver bugle bead. Repeat this bead combination three times on each strand to create a strand of beads. Start attaching a drop pearl to the end of each strand of beads on row 4. Sew and tie off each strand individually. Center the strand just under the first two beads of the last row by catching the fabric on the top of the handbag and make a tiny backstitch. (Do not pull the thread too tightly.) Cut the thread to 3" (8cm) and hand tie a triple knot. Clip the excess thread. Continue in the same manner until the beading pattern is finished.

BEAD PATTERN

◆

row 7 ● ● ● ● ● ● ●
row 6 ● ● ● ● ● ●
row 5 ● ● ● ● ●
row 4 ● ● ● ●
row 3 ● ● ●
row 2 ● ●
row 1 ●

● = equals one strand of beads

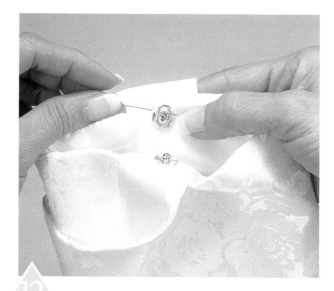

12 Attach the Snap

Center the snap on the inside of the handbag and hand stitch it in place.

Now you have the perfect little handbag to carry with you on your wedding day and beyond. Be creative and try different fabrics to match the style of your dress. This handbag looks gorgeous in silk, taffeta or velvet. In place of the fabric strap, why not try a string of pearls or beads, double-sided satin ribbon or braided cording? Take your cue from your wedding dress and make the handbag you've always wanted.

· tip ·

Want to change the bag after the wedding? Stitch the beading on a square of grosgrain ribbon and secure it to the handbag with a pin back. Remove it later to change the look of the bag.

BEADING ALTERNATIVES

◆

Page 26 shows how to create the elegant hand-beaded design on the front of the handbag. If hand beading feels too labor-intensive for you or you want to try a different look, go to a fabric store and look for premade beaded appliqués that can be hand stitched or hot glued to the front of your bag. Or try a dramatic ribbon rose, silk flower or stylish brooch in place of the beading.

BRIDAL HEADPIECE *and* VEIL

This exquisite headpiece with detachable veil looks stunning but is very simple to make. Just take a plain headband, add a little tulle, ribbon, satin and trimming, pick up your glue gun and you can make a beautiful headpiece and veil for a fraction of the bridal salon price. The best thing about this project is that you can customize it to fit your wedding style. Wear the bun wrap headpiece alone for an informal look or change the length of the veil to match your wedding dress. Check out Choosing the Right Veil on page 31 to design your own veil, from short and sweet to long and dramatic. Design a headpiece and veil that flatters your face, complements your dress and suits your personality. If it feels comfortable and makes you feel beautiful, you know you've picked the right one!

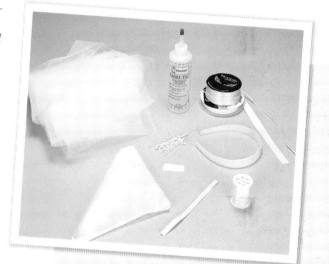

materials:

- ¾" (2cm) wide headband (without teeth)
- ¼ yd. (23cm) satin fabric
- 3 yd. x 19½" (3m x 50cm) tulle
- ⅝" (2cm) wide grosgrain ribbon
- 7" (18cm) of ⅜" (1cm) wide elastic
- fifty pearl stems
- 10 yd. (9m) satin cording
- ¼" (6mm) wide double-sided tape
- Velcro
- white 40 wt. thread
- fabric glue
- hand-sewing needle
- glue gun

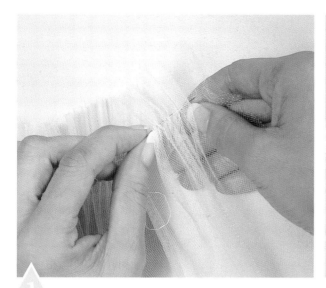

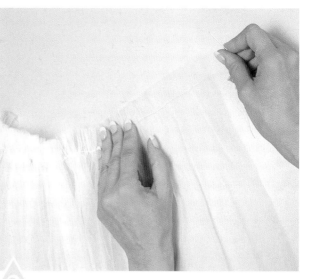

Baste the Tulle

Hand baste a running seam along the entire length of the tulle 1" (3cm) from the top. Do not cut the thread.

Gather the Tulle

To form the veil, tie a knot at one end of the basting thread and pull the thread at the other end of the tulle to gather it until it is only 7" (18cm) wide. Tie the thread and cut off the excess. Set the veil aside.

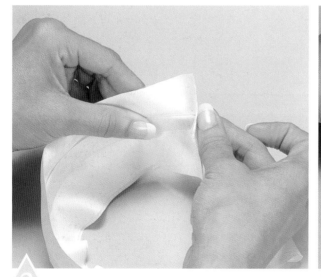

Cut the Fabric

Measure the length of the headband and add approximately 1" (3cm), then measure the width of the headband and add approximately 2" (5cm). Cut the satin fabric to these measurements. Since my headband is 15" x 3/4" (38cm x 2cm), I cut the satin fabric 16" x 3" (41cm x 8cm). Place a small piece of double-sided tape on the inside of the headband at the bottom. Center the fabric on the headband and fold the ends of the fabric over onto the tape. Press the ends flat.

Place the Double-Sided Tape

Place double-sided tape along the center of the inside of the headband from one end to the other.

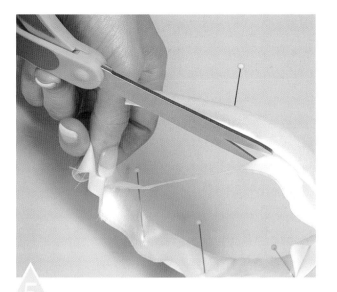

5 Cover the Headband

Fold one side of the fabric onto the tape and press until it is smooth. Trim the excess fabric. Hot glue the ends. Fold the fabric on the other side. Adjust and pin in place. Trim the excess fabric along the edge of the headband.

6 Glue the Fabric

Use only a little hot glue to attach the ends of the satin to the headband. Begin to hot glue the satin into place along the inside length of the headband, removing the pins as you glue. Adjust and trim any excess fabric.

CHOOSING THE RIGHT VEIL

Veils come in all lengths and styles. The edges can be unfinished or trimmed with ribbon or satin cording, and the entire veil can be embellished with sewn-on pearls, crystals, sequins, beads, silk flowers or embroidery. Customize your veil to match the style of your wedding dress by adding decorative details or simply by changing the length. Here is a guide to the different lengths for the veil of your dreams:

Ballet (or waltz) length veils fall somewhere between the knees and the ankles.

Cathedral veils are long and dramatic, falling 3½ yd. (3m) from your headpiece so it trails several feet behind you. Perfect with a dress with or without a cathedral train, you can detach the longer part of the veil during the reception.

Chapel length veils extend to the floor 2½ yds. (2m) from your headpiece so there is just enough fabric to gently pool around your feet.

Elbow length veils fall 25" (64cm) in length to your elbows.

Fingertip veils extend to the end of your fingers. This popular length is particularly beautiful with ball gown styles.

Flyaway veils are multilayered and just barely brush the shoulders. Usually made with stiffened fabric, they slightly lift away from the body. They are also referred to as Madonna veils.

Blusher veils are short, single-layer veils worn over the face to add mystery to your walk down the aisle. They can be worn with any style or length of veil described above.

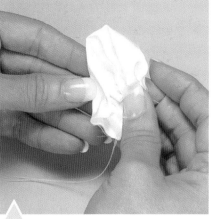

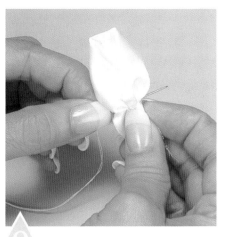

7 Sew Rosebuds

Cut the satin into thirty 2" x 4" (5cm x 10cm) strips. Fold the wrong sides together lengthwise and pin together. Hand baste the fabric in a long U-shape pattern, rounding off the corners as you stitch. Allow a $\frac{1}{4}$" (6mm) seam allowance. Do not cut the thread until the rosebud is complete.

8 Gather and Fold

Pull the thread to gather the fabric together. Overlap the gathers one on top of the other to form a small rosebud.

9 Secure the Rosebud

To secure the rosebud, stitch the base, tightly wrap the thread around the rosebud and tie it off.

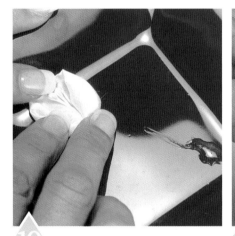

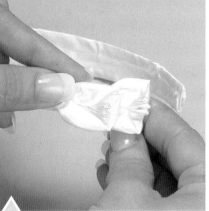

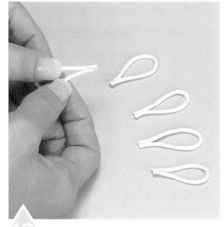

10 Cut the Pearl Stems

Cut approximately forty-five pearl stems in half. Use fabric glue to secure three pearl stems in the center of each rosebud. Repeat steps 7–10 to create thirty rosebuds.

11 Attach the Rosebuds

Begin hot gluing the rosebuds up each side of the headband until they meet in the middle. Overlap each rosebud slightly.

12 Create Cording Loops

Cut forty 3" (8cm) lengths of cording. Make a loop and hot glue the ends together.

13 Attach the Cording Loops

Hot glue a cording loop on each side of every other rosebud, working from each end of the headband up to the center.

14 Attach the Loops to the Center of the Headband

At the center of the headband, hot glue five cording loops on each side so that there are ten loops forming a bow. Cut five pearl stems in half and hot glue one pearl stem to the center of each loop.

· tip ·

You can hot glue loops of cording next to every rose bud if you prefer.

15 Create a Rosebud Center

Hot glue two rosebuds together, end to end. Cut a 3" (8cm) length of cording and hot glue one end to the back of the two rosebuds where their ends intersect. Wrap the cording tightly around the intersection three times. Cut the excess cording and secure the end with hot glue on the back of the rosebuds.

16 Attach the Rosebuds

Place the two rosebuds in the center of the headband and hot glue them into the intersection of the ten loops of cording. Hold the rosebuds in place until the glue has bonded.

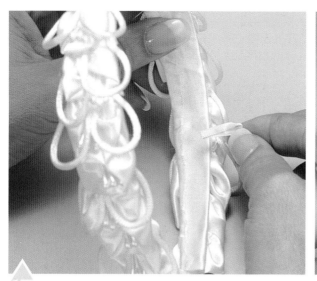

17 Create Hairpin Loops

Cut two 1" (3cm) pieces of satin cording. On each side of the headband, 2½" (6cm) from each end, make a small loop for hairpins and secure with hot glue.

18 Add Grosgrain Ribbon

Place double-sided tape along the inside of the headband from end to end. Cut the grosgrain ribbon to 15" (38cm). Fold the end of the ribbon ½" (1cm) and glue in place. Press the ribbon to the inside of the end of the headband and cut off any excess ribbon. Make sure to keep the hairpin loops free.

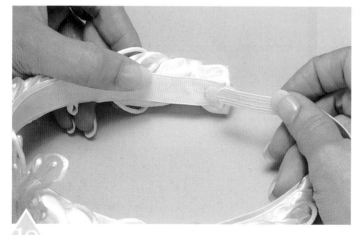

19 Attach the Velcro

Cut two small Velcro circles and hot glue on the inside of the headband at each end. Do not take the Velcro apart. Hot glue each end of the 6½" (17cm) piece of elastic to the Velcro circles to create a detachable veil band. When you have glued the elastic to the Velcro, then you can pull it apart.

20 Attach the Veil

Run a line of hot glue down the middle of the elastic and attach it to the veil. The veil is now easily detachable with the Velcro circles.

here comes the bride!

Take your headpiece and veil with you to your hairstylist to make sure it fits comfortably on your head and complements your hairstyle. Secure the bun wrap headpiece to your head by sliding hairpins through the cording loops on each side. After the ceremony, you can detach the veil and dance until dawn. To create your own variation on this headpiece, embellish the headband with satin or silk flowers, or cover it with beaded lace. Add drama to the veil by edging it with ribbon or lace trim or spraying it with glitter for extra sparkle.

SMOOTHING OUT WRINKLES

To keep your veil looking beautiful until your wedding day, hang it up right away so the entire length hangs freely. In a couple of days any wrinkles will fall out naturally. If you need to get the wrinkles out quickly, hang it in a steamy bathroom. Or you can use a hair dryer on the lowest setting. Hold it 12" (30cm) away from the veil, and move it around a lot so it doesn't overheat or scorch any one spot. Whatever you do, don't take an iron to it, as it may melt the delicate material.

FLOWER GIRL HEADBAND

Crown the head of your charming flower girl with a headband wrapped in satin ribbons and beads. Pair it

with an adorable ballerina-style dress made of tulle, organza or taffeta with ballet slippers or patent leather

shoes to match, and you have the perfect wedding ensemble for your little maid. Offer her a basketful of petals

and watch everyone smile as she walks down the aisle.

materials:

- ¼" (6mm) wide headband (without teeth)
- 4 yd. (4m) of ⅛" (3mm) wide satin ribbon
- 2½ yd. (2m) of ⅜" (1cm) wide picot ribbon
- 4 yd. (4m) of ⅜" (1cm) wide double-sided satin ribbon
- 4 yd. (4m) iridescent pearl strand
- 4 yd. (4m) iridescent cording
- 3mm white pearls
- 3mm crystal beads
- double-sided tape
- 30-gauge wire
- masking tape
- white 40 wt. thread
- extra-fine beading needle
- glue gun

Make the Braid

Cut four lengths of iridescent cording and one strand of iridescent pearls to 23" (58cm) each. Hot glue all the strands together at one end and tape it to the table. Begin to braid by overlapping the two pieces of cording over the pearl strand and then the last two pieces of cording. Do not twist when braiding. Continue braiding and hot glue to secure the end.

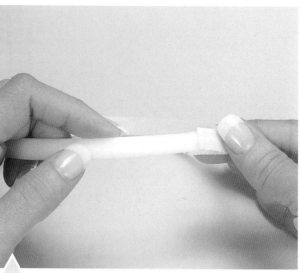

Attach the Ribbon

Place double-sided tape on each end of the headband on both the front and the back. Cut two pieces of ⅜" (1cm) wide double-sided satin ribbon to 2" (5cm) and press them onto the double-sided tape.

Wrap the Headband With Ribbon

Glue ⅜" (1cm) wide double-sided satin ribbon to the back of the headband at one end and begin to wrap the ribbon at an angle around the entire headband, overlapping the ribbon as you go. Cut any excess ribbon and hot glue the ribbon end to the back of the headband.

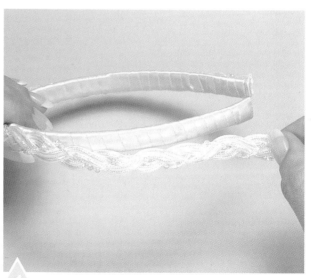

Add the Braid

Attach the braid to one end of the headband with hot glue and continue to glue the braid down every couple of inches until you reach the end of the headband. Secure the end of the braid with hot glue and trim the excess braid.

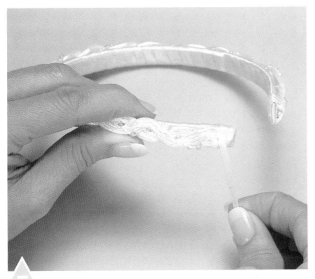

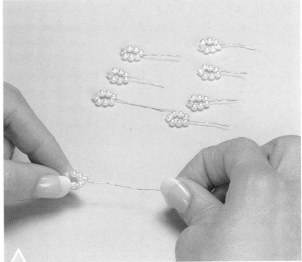

5 Finish the Ends of the Headband

To cover the raw edges of the braid, cut a 5" (13cm) piece of ⅛" (3mm) wide satin ribbon. Hot glue one end of the ribbon to the inside of the headband and wrap the ribbon four or five times around the end of the headband. Hot glue the end of the ribbon to secure it to the back of the headband. Trim any excess ribbon. Repeat for the other side of the headband. Set it aside.

6 Make a Ring of Beads

Cut a 5" (13cm) piece of 30-gauge wire and string three pearls, one crystal bead and three more pearls onto the wire. Twist the wire ends together to form a ring. Keep a 1" (3cm) stem on each ring of beads to avoid any difficulty when gluing it in place. Make approximately twenty rings for the braid and three rings for the bow.

on your wedding day...

When choosing an outfit and accessories for your flower girl, avoid styles and fabrics that are scratchy, stiff or binding. If she feels comfortable and pretty, she'll be less likely to fidget.

7 Glue the Rings of Beads

At each intersection of the braid, insert a ring of beads with a dab of hot glue and hold it in place until the glue is dry.

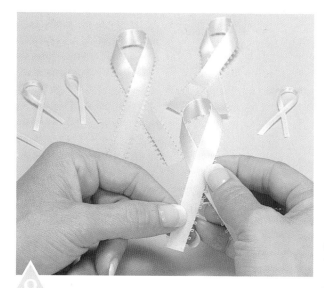

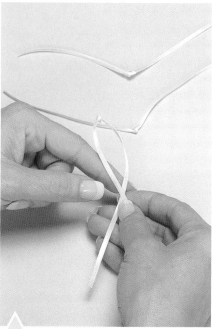

Create Ribbon Loops

Cut three lengths of $\frac{1}{8}$" (3mm) wide satin ribbon to 4" (10cm) each. Overlap the ribbon to form a loop and glue at the center to secure. Repeat this step for each ribbon. Then cut three lengths of $\frac{3}{8}$" (1cm) wide picot ribbon to 11" (28cm) each. Form each ribbon into a loop and hot glue it to secure. Hot glue the three 11" (28cm) loops together in the center, overlapping each loop one on top of the other in a fan shape.

Knot the Loop of Ribbon

Cut three 8" (20cm) lengths of $\frac{1}{8}$" (3mm) wide satin ribbon and tie a knot in the center of each one. Overlap the ends of the ribbon to form a loop and put a dab of glue in the center of the loop to secure.

Attach the Ribbon Loops

Hot glue the 11" (28cm) loops behind and in between the 8" (20cm) loops. Stagger the loops of ribbon and glue them to the middle of the bow in a fan shape.

Attach the Small Ribbon Loops

Hot glue the three 4" (10cm) loops into a fan in the middle of the other loops of ribbon from step 10.

12 **Trim the Ribbon Ends**

Cut all of the ribbon ends at an angle to different lengths. Hot glue three bead rings from step 6 to the center of the bow.

13 **Make Strings of Beads**

With an extra-fine beading needle and thread, enter the back center of the bow and come through the front of the bow. String four crystal beads and three pearls onto the thread and re-enter the front of the bow and out the back. Tie off the thread to secure. Repeat until you have three small dangles of beads in the middle of the bow.

crowning glory

To complete your headband, hot glue the bow to the outside of the headband about 2" (5cm) from the end. As a variation, cover the satin-covered band with small ribbon roses or silk flowers or simply hot glue a flat bow made of satin, velvet or grosgrain ribbon that coordinates with the flower girl's dress. Whatever embellishment you choose, make sure it is in proportion to her small head so it doesn't overpower her face or distract from her dress.

PEARL BARRETTE

Bridesmaids, flower girls and informal brides can dress up their hair with ribbons and pearls secured to inexpensive barrettes for a romantic hair accessory. Perfect for gathering long tresses or adding the perfect accent to an elegant updo, this barrette is easy to make and even easier to customize to your wedding style. Add as much or as little embellishment as you like to match the style of your dress.

materials:

- 2" (5cm) barrette
- 2½ yd. (2m) of ⅛" (3mm) wide satin ribbon
- 1½ yd. (1m) pearl strand
- two pearl sprays
- 4mm pearls
- small pearl appliqué
- ten 5mm iridescent sequins (OPTIONAL)
- 24-gauge wire
- white 40 wt. thread
- glue gun

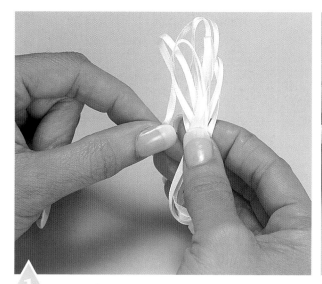

1 Form a Bow

Cut the satin ribbon to 45" (1m). Hold the ribbon between your thumb and index finger and make a loop on each side of your thumb. Continue making loops until there are eight loops on each side.

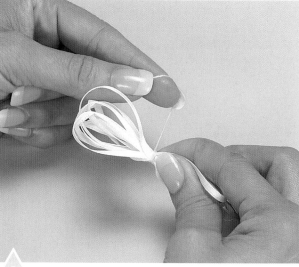

2 Secure the Loops in the Bow

Wrap the center of the bow four times with thread and tie it tightly. Cut any excess thread.

3 Create the Streamer

Cut one 12" (30cm) length of satin ribbon and one 7" (18cm) strand of pearls. Fold both pieces in half and tie them together in the center with a 2½" (6cm) strip of satin ribbon.

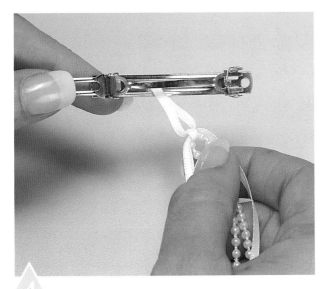

4

Attach the Streamer

Hot glue the short lengths of satin ribbon just under the top bar of the barrette's center to attach the streamer.

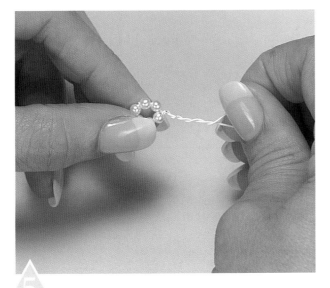

5

Create Pearl Rings

Cut seven 4" (10cm) pieces of 24-gauge wire. String six 4mm pearls to each piece of wire and twist the ends of the wire together to form a ring.

IDEAS FOR HAIR ACCENTS

◆

Some hair accessories look better with either long or short hair. Choose the one that's best for you based on your hairstyle and wedding gown.

Headbands: For short hair, choose something narrow, like a jeweled metal headband. If you have long hair, try a wider band of satin or silk, or one decorated with beads or flowers. See the Flower Girl Headband on page 36 for more headband ideas.

Tiaras: Encrusted with rhinestones, jeweled stones or crystals, tiaras look great with long and short hair.

Hair Combs and Pins: Grab your glue gun and decorate them with beads, pearls, rhinestones, feathers or whatever strikes your fancy. Small combs and hairpins look great with short hair. If you have long hair, center large combs at the crown of the head.

Barrettes and Hair Clips: Perfect for long hair, decorate barrettes or banana clips with sprays, pearls, ribbons or flowers. For an elegant updo or a wispy bun, try hair picks (hair chopsticks) for that extra-special touch to wedding-day hair.

Hats: From pillbox to wide-brimmed, hats look best on short-haired brides. This is also a popular alternative for second-time brides. Decorate with flowers or add tulle for an alternative veil.

Single Flower or Bow: A fresh or silk flower or single bow can be pinned on the back or side of the head. Add narrow ribbons tied with love knots that trail as long as you like. Another option is to add a tuft of tulle netting 6"–10" (15cm x 25cm) long gathered at the base of the flower or bow, or a longer strip that floats along the floor.

Hair Wreaths: Use floral tape to help twist silk or fresh flowers into a hair wreath. For extra romance, add trailing ribbons.

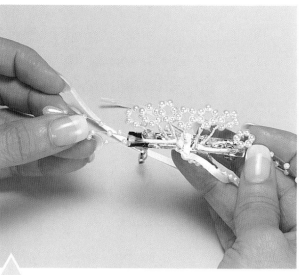

Glue the Pearl Rings

Hot glue seven pearl rings to the top bar of the barrette in a fan shape.

Attach the Pearl Sprays

Cut the pearl spray to the desired length and hot glue one pearl spray to each end of the barrette.

Attach the Bow

Center bow loops on top of the barrette and wrap them with an 8" (20cm) piece of wire. Wrap the wire around the barrette and bow, in between the pearl rings, to secure the bow to the barrette. Add a drop of hot glue to secure it.

Add Embellishment

Hot glue the small pearl appliqué to the center of the bow. If you'd like, use tweezers to place ten 5mm iridescent sequins around the appliqué.

◆

Start the day with your hair a little higher, wider and more done than you're accustomed to. By the time you get to the reception, you will be lucky if it looks styled at all. But remember that people are less interested in seeing your new hairdo than your face.

1. Don't overdo it! Make sure your hair doesn't compete with your gown for attention.

2. If you want to do something different with your hair on your wedding day, visit your hairstylist weeks or months in advance to experiment and prevent any last-minute disasters.

3. If you plan to remove your headpiece and veil after the ceremony, let down your hair or change clothes, you may want to have a hairstylist on-site to do touch-ups after the ceremony.

4. Don't be talked into a hairstyle for your wedding day that's not right for you. Make sure your hairstyle fits your personality and the style of your dress.

5. If you are wearing a headpiece, find a sure-fire way to attach it to your hair. Test the staying power of your headpiece before your wedding day.

6. Wear a button-down shirt when you go to have your hair (and makeup) done so you don't have to pull anything over your head when you change.

add some sparkle and imagination!

Tie love knots randomly on the ribbons and hot glue ten iridescent sequins under the pearls around the pearl appliqué, if desired. If you prefer a simpler version of this barrette, think of your base barrette as a blank canvas. Make a row of small ribbons tied in bows and tie random love knots. Let the ends drape down as long as you like. Or you can hot glue ribbon roses, silk, dried or fresh flowers or a classic flat bow to the barrette. Try gluing a striking brooch or antique buttons for a different look. Have fun and experiment—try a barrette with white shells for a beach wedding or soft feathers for a contemporary look. The possibilities are endless!

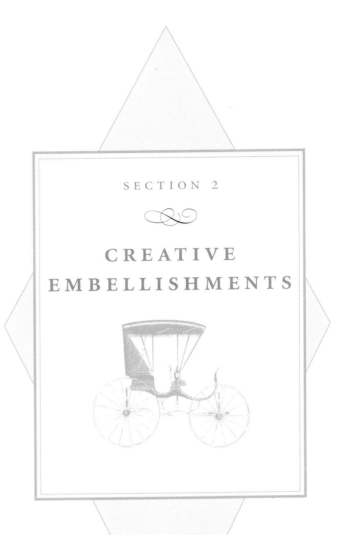

SECTION 2

CREATIVE EMBELLISHMENTS

Think no one will notice the little things like hosiery, gloves or shoes? Think again. It's the details that make an ensemble complete. Add your unique touch to ready-to-wear items, and look elegant in one-of-a-kind designs for your special day.

Start with a plain object, like white gloves or shoes, and add your favorite decoration. From ribbons and flowers to beads and trim, embellishments are a perfect and inexpensive way to coordinate all your wedding accessories. Be creative with adding personal touches to your accessories and let your individual style shine through.

WEDDING GLOVES · BRIDAL HOSIERY · BRIDAL SHOES · FLOWER GIRL SHOES · FLOWER GIRL SOCKS

WEDDING GLOVES

What could be more elegant than finishing off your wedding ensemble with a glamorous pair of gloves? No matter which length you choose, gloves add a romantic touch of sophistication to any wedding gown. Choose a style, fabric and length that complements your dress. Choose from a wide range of fabrics including kid leather, satin spandex, nylon, lace, crochet, crushed velvet, cotton, or sheer organza. Wear your gloves plain or embellish them with beads, ribbon, lace, pearls, sequins or silk flowers. All you need is a needle and thread and you can easily embellish a plain pair of store-bought gloves. Here are three different styles to choose from to help you design the perfect gloves for you.

project one
CUT-AWAY APPLIQUÉ GLOVES

materials:

- wrist-length satin stretch gloves
- 4" x 4" (10cm x 10cm) white tulle
- two white bridal lace appliques
- 1½ yds (1m) of 1" (3cm) wide white sheer ribbon with pearls
- 6" (15cm) satin rattail cording
- white 40 wt. thread
- hand-sewing needle
- embroidery scissors
- glue gun
- cardboard (OPTIONAL)

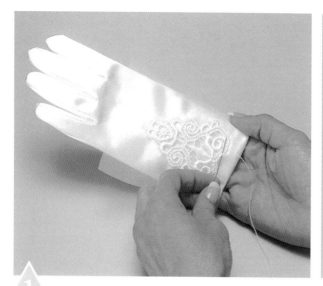

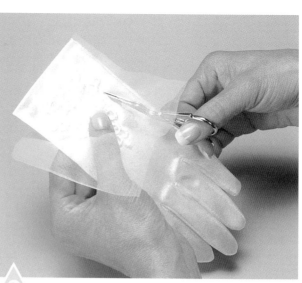

1 Sew the Tulle and Applique

With the lace appliqué on top of the tulle square, center both of them onto the glove and pin in place. Sew the tulle and appliqué to the glove following the outline of the appliqué.

2 Trim the Tulle

With the embroidery scissors, trim away the excess tulle from around the appliqué. Be careful not to cut into the appliqué or the glove.

• tip •

Insert a small square of cardboard into the glove to prevent sewing through the glove.

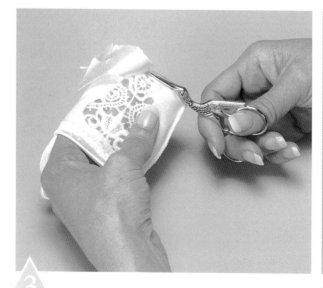

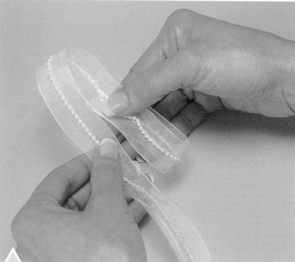

3 Cut Out the Glove

Turn the glove inside out and pull the glove fabric away from the appliqué and tulle. Using the embroidery scissors, carefully cut the glove fabric away from around the inside of the stitch line following the appliqué line.

4 Make Bow Loops

Cut a 20" (51cm) piece of 1" (3cm) wide sheer ribbon with pearls. Hold the ribbon between the thumb and index finger. Make a loop on each side of your thumb. To form four loops, hand gather the ribbon along the center of the bow. Pull and wrap the thread tightly around the center of the bow. Cut the thread and tie it securely.

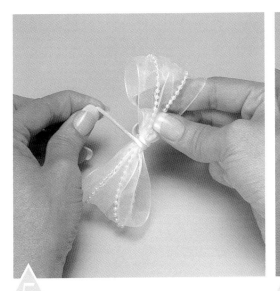

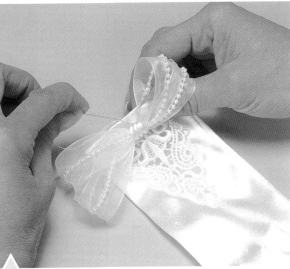

5 **Add Satin Cording**

Cut 4"(10cm) of rattail satin cording and hot glue it to the back of the bow. Wrap the cording snugly around the center of the bow three times and glue the end of the cording to the center back of the bow. Cut away any excess cording.

6 **Secure the Bow to the Glove**

Center the bow on the wrist of the glove and hand stitch it to the wrist of the glove. Clip the thread and tie it securely.

GLOVE GLOSSARY

Fingerless Gloves: Worn short or long, these gloves make it easy to exchange rings.

Gauntlet Gloves: Looking more like a sleeve, these gloves have no fingers or hands and stop at the elbow.

Wrist Gloves: Perfect for informal or semi-formal weddings, these gloves end at the wrist.

Elbow Gloves: Stopping just above or below the elbow, these gloves have six to ten buttons depending on the length of your arm.

Opera Gloves: These formal gloves stop at the middle of your upper arm and have fourteen to sixteen buttons.

WHAT GLOVE GOES WITH WHAT SLEEVE?

Sleeveless or strapless: over-the-elbow-length glove

Short sleeve: below-the-elbow-length glove

Long sleeve: wrist-length glove

take my hand...

If Audrey Hepburn in *Breakfast at Tiffany's* is your inspiration, these are the perfect gloves for you. When choosing embellished gloves like these, make sure your gloves don't detract from the beauty of your gown. Wear plain or minimally embellished gloves with an ornate gown and more embellished gloves with a simply styled gown.

DIFFICULTY:

project two

BRIDAL BEADED TRIM GLOVES

materials:

- wrist-length nylon stretch gloves
- 1 yd. (9m) white bridal beaded trim
- white 40 wt. thread
- hand-sewing needle
- embroidery scissors

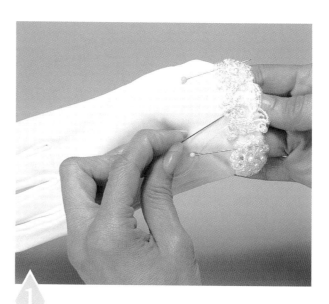

1 Sew on Bridal Trim

Pin the beaded trim to the wrist of the glove (top side only). Cut the excess trim and hand stitch it securely to the glove.

GLOVES ON OR OFF?

KEEP YOUR GLOVES ON:

- walking up and down the aisle
- first dance with your new husband, father and father-in-law
- wedding pictures

TAKE YOUR GLOVES OFF:

- in the receiving line
- while eating or drinking
- signing the marriage license
- cutting the wedding cake
- during makeup touch-ups

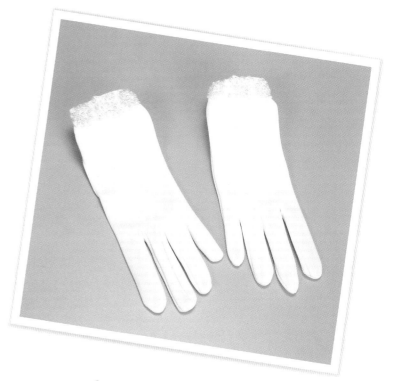

beaded glamour...

Beaded trimming looks good on just about everything. Try using it on shoes, pants, hats or handbags.

all out glamour...

For sheer drama at a formal evening wedding, these beaded elbow gloves will add sparkle as you float down the aisle. If you fall in love with a pair of hand-beaded gloves like these, but can't afford the bridal salon price, don't fear for your budget. You can make your own glamorous beaded gloves without the less-than-glamorous bridal salon price. All it takes is a little patience to bead an inexpensive pair of plain gloves.

WITH THIS RING...

During the ceremony you need to find a way to expose your ring finger. If you are wearing short gloves, you can take your gloves off altogether and hand them to your maid of honor. Before you walk back down the aisle, put your gloves back on. Practice taking them on and off before the wedding so you are not struggling and fumbling at the alter. With longer gloves, you can choose fingerless gloves or make a small slit along the seam of your ring finger. If you choose the latter, simply slide your ring finger out and tuck the loose glove finger inside your glove.

BRIDAL HOSIERY

Look great coming and going by wearing delicately embellished hosiery that complements your wedding gown. A small beaded appliqué on your ankle is a chic accent when you gracefully lift your gown to descend from your limousine or horse-drawn carriage. Or decorate sexy stockings with seams with a tiny, feminine bow for that extra touch of style. No matter what small accent you choose, keep it simple so it doesn't distract from your gown, tear your hose or feel unnatural on your legs.

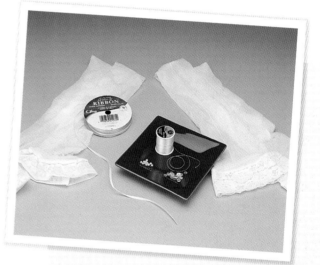

project one
RIBBON AND PEARL STOCKINGS

materials:

- stockings with seam
- small piece of cardboard
- ⅛" (3mm) wide satin ribbon
- two 2mm pearls
- two 5mm clear sequins
- white 40 wt. thread
- hand-sewing needle

on your wedding day...

Hosiery is available in many shades of white to match the range of shades in wedding fabrics. Choose sheer hose in a shade that complements your dress. For a little extra glamour, choose hosiery with a slight sheen or sparkle.

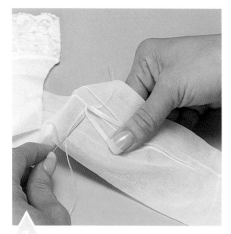

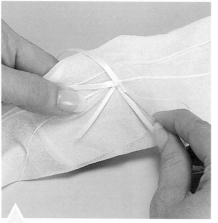

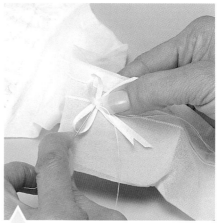

Create the Streamer

Insert a small piece of cardboard into the stocking. Cut 3½" (9cm) of ⅛" (3mm) wide satin ribbon, fold it in half and sew the center of the ribbon into the seam line of the stocking about 12" (30cm) to 15" (38cm) up from the toe depending on shoe size. Don't cut the thread until all the steps are finished.

Position the Second Ribbon

Cut 7" (18cm) of satin ribbon. Sew the center of the ribbon on top of the 3½" (9cm) ribbon.

Make the Bow

Fold one end of the 7" (18cm) satin ribbon over to make a loop. Make a stitch in the center to secure. Repeat for the other side of the bow.

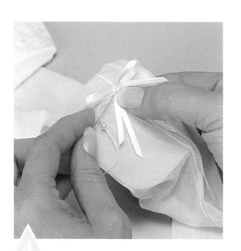

Add the Sequin and Pearl

Place a sequin and a pearl onto the thread in the center of the bow and stitch to secure it.

sheerly appealing!

In addition to bows, you can embellish seams by attaching rhinestones with fabric glue or hand stitching flat-back beads or pearls. If you choose to wear thigh-highs or garter stockings, try them on with your wedding ensemble before your wedding day to make sure they don't cause unwanted bulges and will stay up through dancing at the reception.

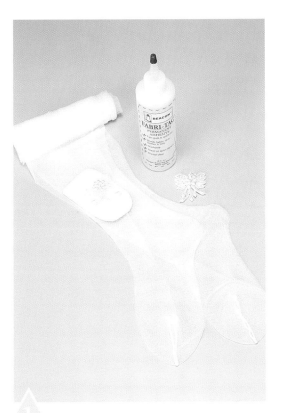

materials:

- panty hose
- two small bridal appliqués
- small piece of cardboard
- fabric glue

Apply the Appliqué

Insert a small piece of cardboard into the stocking. Glue the bridal appliqué to the outside ankle of the stocking about 10½" (27cm) to 12" (30cm) from the toe. Do not remove the cardboard until the glue is dry.

sparkle from head to toe!

Test out the combination of your slip or crinoline with your hose, especially if your hose has any embellishment. The friction between the two against your legs could end up shredding them, so try on your hose and slip on your crinoline before your wedding day.

DIFFICULTY:

BRIDAL SHOES

Do you want designer shoes without designer prices? Design them yourself! Purchase plain pumps, slippers or sandals, get your glue gun and a needle and thread and start creating the perfect wedding shoes. In no time a small amount of ribbon, beads and lace can transform an ordinary pair of shoes into fabulous slippers fit for a princess. Be sure to design a shoe that complements your dress and fits your style. Elaborate dresses do not need elaborate shoes, while more simple dresses look great with more embellished shoes.

project one
1 PEARL-EDGED SHOE

1 Attach the Organza Edge

At the center in the back of the shoe, begin to hot glue the pearl organza edge just inside the shoe's top edge. Trim the excess organza at the back of the shoe to allow the edge to lie flat.

2 Form the Bow

Cut a 23" (58cm) length of ribbon and with one end of the ribbon free, make a 3" (8cm) loop for the center of the bow, holding the ribbon between your thumb and index finger. Continue making loops on each side of your thumb. Each loop should be 2" (5cm) bigger than the last one, for a total of six loops, three loops on each side of the center loop.

3 Secure the Bow

Holding the bow together in the center with your fingers, wrap the thread tightly around all but the center loop. Knot the thread and cut any excess.

4 Attach the Teardrop Pearl

Hot glue the bow to the back center of the shoe and stitch a teardrop pearl just under the center of the bow.

materials:

- 2 yd. (2m) of 1" (3cm) wide double-sided satin ribbon
- 1½ yd. (1m) pearl organza ribbon
- two 1" (3cm) teardrop pearls with ring
- white 40 wt. thread
- hand-sewing needle
- glue gun

SATIN ROSETTE SHOE WITH PEARL BOW

DIFFICULTY:

materials:

- 1 yd. (1m) of 1" (3cm) wide sheer ribbon with pearl
- 2 yd. (2m) of $\frac{1}{2}$" (1cm) wide double-sided satin wired ribbon
- shoe clip
- white 40 wt. thread
- hand-sewing needle
- glue gun

1 Make the Satin Bow

Cut an 11" (28cm) length of wired satin ribbon and mark the center. Form bow loops by bringing each ribbon end to the center and overlap the end $\frac{1}{4}$" (6mm). Hand stitch in the center of the ribbon to secure the loops but do not cut the thread.

2 Make the Sheer Bow

Cut a 20" (51cm) length of sheer ribbon. Leaving one end free for a 3" (8cm) streamer, hold the ribbon between your thumb and index finger. Form a loop on each side of the satin bow loop. Hand stitch to secure the loops using the same thread. Pull the thread to gather the ribbon in the center. Wrap the thread around the bow a few times to secure. Tie a knot and cut any excess thread.

3 Make the Rosette

Create a rosette using 20" (51cm) length of the wired satin ribbon as described in the sidebar on the facing page. Position the rosette in the center of the sheer bow and hot glue it into place.

4 Add the Shoe Clip

Hand stitch the shoe clip to the center back of the bow. Cut the thread and tie a triple knot. Clip it to the shoe.

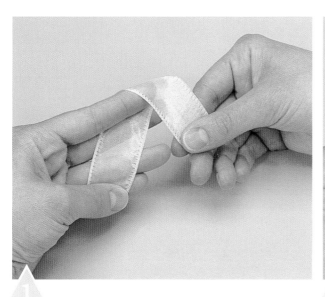

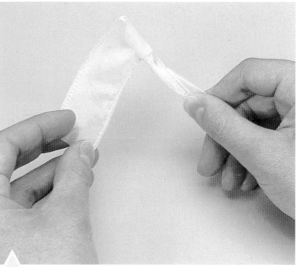

1 Cut your ribbon to 20" (51cm) and fold the right end of the ribbon down 2" (5cm) to form a stem.

2 Roll the ribbon four times to form the center of the rosette. Make a stitch at the base of the rosette to secure it.

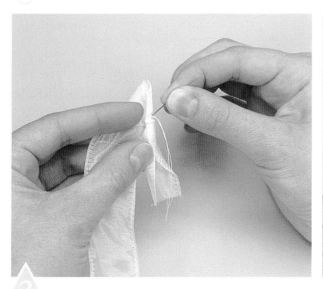

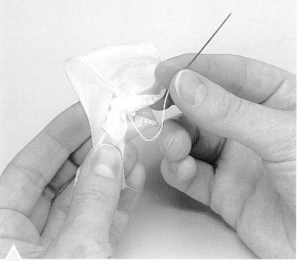

3 Fold the ribbon back to the left and turn the rosette once. Stitch the center to secure the rosette but don't cut the thread yet. Continue folding and turning the ribbon until the rosette is the size you want. Secure the rosette with a stich at every turn.

4 Secure the end of the rosette by folding the end. Stitch or glue it in place with a small amount of hot glue. Cut the excess ribbon.

FLOWER GIRL SHOES

From patent leather to ballet flats, you can create one-of-a-kind shoes to make any flower girl feel special. To keep your flower girl from slipping and sliding down the aisle, scuff the bottom of her shoes or put a strip of duct tape on the bottom to give her a little traction. Try these embellishment ideas on shoes for the bride and bridesmaids, too!

PEARL BRAID AND ROSETTE SHOES

1 Glue the Pearl Braid

Hot glue the braid to the front center of the shoe and follow the edge all the way around. Trim the excess braid and glue the ends flat.

2 Make Ribbon Loops

Cut a 10" (25cm) length of picot ribbon, make a 4" (10cm) loop and glue the loop to secure. Fold the ribbon back on itself and repeat two more times, while securing each loop with hot glue. Make each loop 1" (3cm) shorter than the previous loop. Hot glue it onto the top of the braid at the front center of the shoe.

3 Make the Pearl Ring

Cut a 3" (8cm) piece of wire and thread on six pearls. Twist the ends of the wire tightly and lay it aside.

4 Make the Ribbon Rosette

Cut a 15" (38cm) length of picot ribbon and create a rosette as described on page 63. Hot glue the pearl ring and rosette to the toe of the shoe.

materials list

- 1½ yd. (1m) of ½" (1cm) wide picot ribbon
- 1½ yd. (1m) of ½" (1cm) wide pearl braid
- twelve 3mm pearls
- 30-gauge bead wire
- white 40 wt. thread
- hand-sewing needle
- glue gun

variation:
ROSETTE APPLIQUÉ SHOES

fast **and** fabulous!

Want something quick and easy? Go to the fabric or craft store and find beaded appliqués like this rosette. Hot glue one to the toe of each shoe, using very little glue on the outside edge of the appliqué to avoid staining the shoe fabric.

FLOWER GIRL SOCKS

What little miss wouldn't be proud to wear pretty socks embellished beyond the limits of sweetness, trimmed with guipure lace and baby pearls on the cuff or sparkling with a beaded pearl appliqué? Flower girl socks are easy to personalize and embellish, and they make a special gift for your little maid. You can use any kind of delicate trim, lace, small appliqué or beading to accent ankle socks. Take your cue from the fabric and details on her dress and the style of her shoes. Keep the embellishment simple to keep the focus on her sweet face as she sprinkles blossoms down the aisle.

LACE TRIM SOCKS

materials list

• ankle socks
• 1 yd. (1m) lace trim
• 3mm pearls
• white 40 wt. thread
• hand-sewing needle

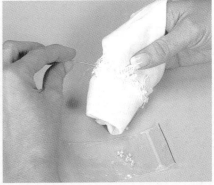

1 Pin the Lace
Pin the lace trim around the edge of the sock cuff. Overlap the lace trim at the end and cut off the excess. Hand stitch the lace trim around the cuff.

2 Sew the Pearls
Sew a pearl to the lace trim, one at a time. Clip and tie off the thread ends securely. Following the pattern of the lace trim, continue placing the pearls according to your preference.

variation:
APPLIQUÉ SOCKS

fast and fabulous!

This quick and easy project requires two pearl appliqués. Center each appliqué accurately on the sock cuff and pin it in place. Hand stitch around the outside edge of the appliqué. Make sure you sew only the cuff of the sock and not the whole sock together. Clip and tie the thread ends securely.

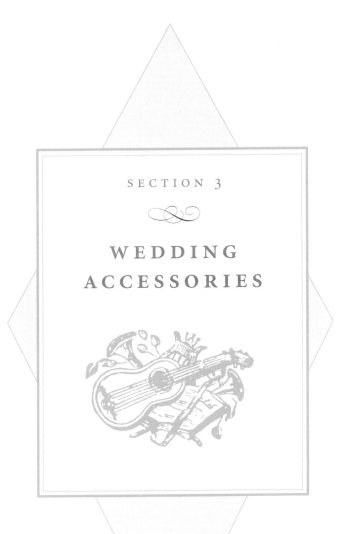

SECTION 3

WEDDING
ACCESSORIES

Now that your ensemble is complete with accessories and special extras, there are still a few more areas you can make unique with your personalized touch, including articles used in the ceremony and reception. And by specially crafting these items, you can tailor all the wedding necessities from unity candles to toasting flutes to your color scheme and overall wedding theme without spending a lot of money.

Forget the engraver. You can easily personalize your cake servers and toasting flutes yourself. Ribbons, lace, pearls and beads can turn inexpensive plain servers and flutes into very special works of art.

RING BEARER PILLOW · LACE FLOWER GIRL BASKET · UNITY CANDLE · CAKE KNIFE & SERVER · TOASTING FLUTES

RING BEARER PILLOW

Create a beautiful keepsake ring pillow featuring your wedding invitation that you will cherish long after your wedding day. This simple pillow made of white satin is easy to make. For embellishment, add a clear vinyl pocket outlined in pearl trim for your invitation and delicate satin ribbons to tie on your rings and you will have something completely personal and unique for your wedding ceremony. Choose from a variety of luxurious bridal fabrics to design your pillow including silk shantung, moiré, velvet, organza and lace. Add your own special touches that reflect your wedding style from accents of silk or fresh flowers, tassels, small ribbon roses or whatever your heart desires.

materials:

- ½ yd. (46cm) satin fabric
- bridal pearl trim
- bridal rose appliqué
- ¼" (6mm) wide sheer satin ribbon
- ⅛" (3mm) wide satin ribbon
- poly fiber–fill
- quilt batting
- 16-gauge clear vinyl plastic or light weight clear plastic vinyl
- wedding invitation
- white 40 wt. thread
- glue gun
- tape

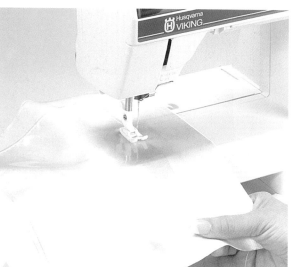

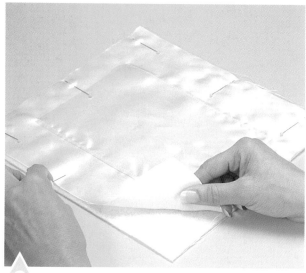

1 Sew the Plastic to the Satin Fabric

Cut two 11" x 11" (28cm x 28cm) squares of satin fabric and one 11" x 11" (28cm x 28cm) square of quilt batting. Cut the clear plastic 1" (3cm) larger on all sides than your invitation. Center the plastic on the right side of the satin fabric and tape it down. Sew the plastic to the fabric on three sides leaving the top side open so the invitation can be inserted later. Do not sew over the tape. Remove each piece of tape as you sew.

2 Pin the Quilt Batting

Pin the square of quilt batting to the wrong side of the satin fabric with the plastic sewn to it.

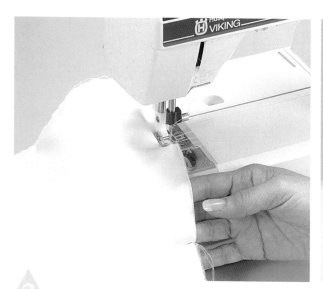

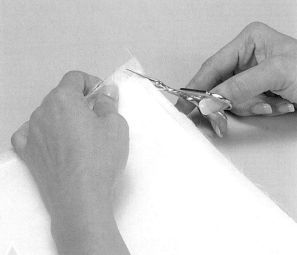

3 Sew the Pillow

With the right sides of the satin fabric facing each other, pin the squares together. Stitch around the pillow using a ¼" (6mm) seam allowance. Leave a 6" (15cm) opening on one side for turning inside out and stuffing the pillow.

4 Cut the Corners

Cut all the corners diagonally. Trim the seam allowance and turn the pillow right side out. Press the pillow with a cool iron if necessary.

Glue the Pearl Trim

Hot glue the pearl trim around the edges of the plastic to cover up the stitching lines on the plastic. Put the hot glue on the back of the trim to avoid melting the plastic.

· tip ·

To prevent the hot glue from getting on the fabric at the top edge of the plastic, insert a small piece of paper into the pillow pocket.

Attach the Streamers

Cut a 22" (56cm) piece of sheer satin ribbon. Cut a 22$\frac{1}{4}$" (57cm) and a 14" (36cm) piece of satin ribbon. Fold all three ribbons in the center, and glue them to the top left corner of the plastic on the edge of the pearl trim. Randomly tie slip knots along the streamers and tie on the wedding rings.

Tie a Shoestring Bow

Cut two 14" (36cm) lengths of sheer satin ribbon, and tie a shoestring bow. Repeat with the $\frac{1}{8}$" (3mm) wide satin ribbon. Glue both to the top left corners of the pillow over the streamers. Trim the ribbon ends diagonally.

Add the Ribbon Loops

Cut two 4" (10cm) pieces of the sheer satin and satin ribbons. Make ribbon loops and glue the ends together with just a dab of hot glue. Attach the loops one on top of the other at the center of the bow with hot glue.

9 ◆ Attach the Rose

Cut one small rose from the pearl trim and hot glue it to the center of the bow.

10 ◆ Add the Bridal Appliqué

At the center of the pillow top just above the plastic, glue the bridal appliqué onto the fabric.

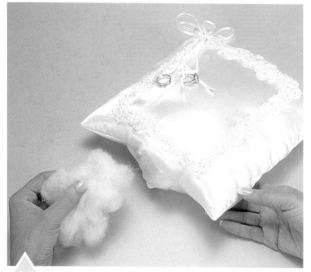

11 ◆ Stuff the Pillow

Use poly fiber-fill to stuff the pillow. Stuff the corners of the pillow first. Use small amounts of poly fiber-fill and fill the pillow gradually. This will keep the pillow from looking lumpy.

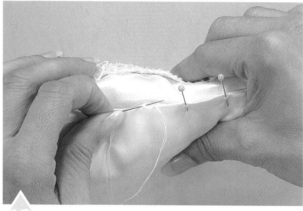

12 ◆ Close the Opening

Slip stitch the opening in the pillow closed. Tie the ends of the thread together and cut excess thread.

· tip ·

Give your ring bearer a set of symbolic rings for his trip down the aisle and the real rings to your maid or matron of honor and the best man.

The text on the pillow reads:

This day I will marry my best friend,
Lisa G. Brewer
daughter of
Mr. & Mrs. Edwin Brewer
and
Christopher C. Carson
son of
Mr. & Mrs. Homer L. Carson
on Saturday, the ninth of December
two thousand and one
at three o'clock in the afternoon
Mt. Moriah Church
129 Crestview Ave.
Florence, Ky. 45776

With this ring I thee wed...

To complete your keepsake ring pillow, insert the wedding invitation into the plastic pocket and tie the rings on the streamers. To create variations on this pillow, you can change the fabric or trim or replace the invitation with a copy of your marriage license or a wedding photo after the wedding. You can also make the pillow in the shape of a heart instead of a square.

VARIATION

• ring pillow with bow

Here's an easy variation! Wrap your pillow in wide, wired ribbon and tie a large bow. Hold the ribbon in place with a few stitches on the underside of the pillow. Add a large silk or ribbon rose in the center of the bow for added drama. For a softer bow, use double-sided satin or organza ribbon. Don't forget to add the ribbons for tying on your rings.

on your wedding day...

Ring bearers are usually between the ages of four and eight and typically walk down the aisle before or alongside the flower girl. Remember that part of the charm of having children in your wedding is their unpredictability. Talk to your little helper about the events that will take place before and throughout the wedding day. This will help him visualize his role and cut down on wedding day jitters. Invite him and his parents to the rehearsal so he can practice walking down the aisle several times. Also make sure his parents are seated on the aisle so he will see familiar faces to help him feel more comfortable.

LACE FLOWER GIRL BASKET

For a stylish twist on the traditional flower girl basket, you can create a lace fabric basket lined with sheer organza and accented with tulle, pearls, ribbon and rhinestones for extra sparkle. Fill the basket with fresh, silk or dried petals, confetti or potpourri. Coordinate the lace fabric of the basket with your little maid's dress and pick up decorative accents and colors from your wedding to embellish the basket with your own special touch. For more flower girl accessories you can make, see the flower girl headband on page 36, embellishments for flower girl shoes on page 64 and decorative accents for flower girl socks on page 66.

materials:

- ½ yd. (46cm) Alençon lace
- ½ yd. (46cm) sheer organza (for basket lining)
- ½ yd. (46cm) of ½" (6mm) wide ivory satin ribbon
- ½ yd. (23cm) shiny tulle
- ½ yd. (46cm) 3mm pearl strand
- 4 yd. (4m) 4mm pearl strand
- 1½ yd. (1m) rattail cording
- 3mm pearls
- flat-back rhinestones
- tissue paper
- spray stiffener
- bead glue (or fabric glue specifying use for beads)
- white 40 wt. thread
- hand-sewing needle

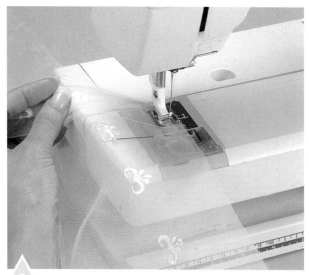

1 Sew the Bottom Seam

Pin the Alençon lace and organza together to cut as one piece of fabric. Cut a 16" x 16" (41cm x 41cm) square. With right sides together, stitch a $\frac{1}{4}$" (6mm) seam line along the end opposite the scallop edge. Trim the fabric to $\frac{1}{8}$" (3mm) seam allowance.

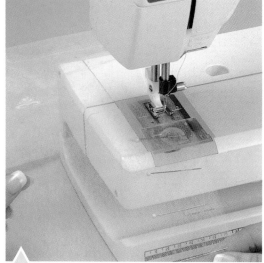

2 Sew the Side Seam

Open up the fabric and fold it lengthwise with the right sides of the fabric together. Stitch a $\frac{1}{4}$" (6mm) seam line. Trim the fabric to a $\frac{1}{8}$" (3mm) seam allowance.

on your wedding day...

During the processional, flower girls walk directly in front of the bride and maid of honor. During the ceremony, young flower girls can either stand with the bridesmaids or sit with their family.

3 Turning the Fabric

Turn the fabric right side out with the organza lining on the inside. Finger press the bottom seam flat.

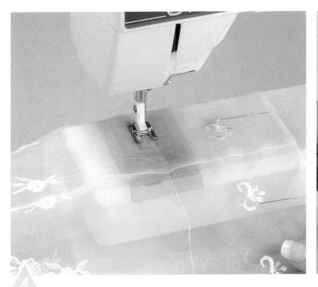

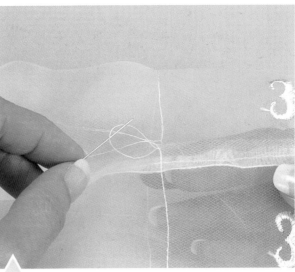

Baste the Fabric

On your sewing machine, baste stitch the basket 4" (10cm) from the bottom edge, leaving the thread around 3" (8cm) long. This will be gathered later.

Pull Up the Threads

Pull up all four threads from your baste stitch to the outside of the fabric at the seam. Do not cut the threads.

CHOOSING A FLOWER GIRL

• The best age range for flower girls is between four and eight. But don't forget to take her personality into account as well as her age. An outgoing four-year-old may be a better choice than a shy eight-year-old.

• Communicate clearly with your flower girl leading up to the wedding. Be open to her suggestions and concerns. And let her know that it is okay if she changes her mind about being in your wedding.

• Invite your flower girl to your wedding shower and other pre-wedding parties if appropriate. Make sure she attends the rehearsal and the rehearsal dinner with her family if possible.

• Practice her routine several times before the wedding day, complete with her outfit, accessories and flower basket. On the wedding day, seat her parents and other familiar faces along the aisle to help ease her nerves.

• Don't forget to show your appreciation to your flower girl by giving her a small gift to thank her for being a part of your special day.

Add Rhinestones and Pearls

Use bead glue to place rhinestones and 3mm pearls throughout the lace design. Use only a very small amount of bead glue. Use a straight pin to pick up the pearls, allow the pearls to slide down the pin into the glue, and press to secure.

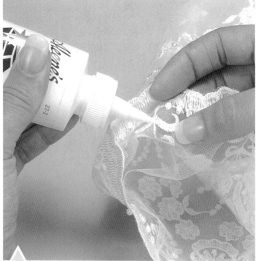

Glue the Lining

Run a small line of glue between the lace and organza. Press both together and let dry.

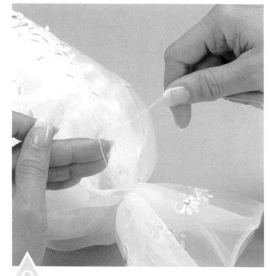

Shape the Basket

Insert large balls of tissue paper to shape the basket. Pull the thread to gather the bottom, wrapping threads around the gathered base. Tie the ends of the thread in a knot to secure and cut any excess thread.

Make the Braid

Cut two strands of cording and one pearl strand (choose either the 3mm or 4mm strand) to 25" (64cm) each. Glue the three ends together and tape to the table. Braid the strands together and glue the ends to secure.

⑩ Attach the Braid Handle

With the seam in front of you, glue each end of the handle on the inside of the basket on either side of the seam. Adjust the handle if it is too long.

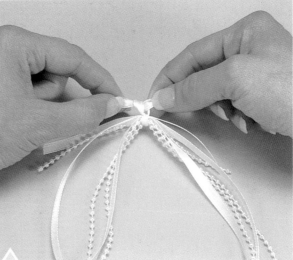

⑪ Make the Streamers

Cut three strands of satin ribbon to 30" (76cm), 12" (30cm), and 8" (20cm). Cut three pearl strands (either the 3mm or 4mm) the same lengths. Fold all ribbon and pearl strands in half and tie them tightly with 4" (10cm) satin ribbon.

· tip ·

You may want to add a small amount of glue to your knot. This will keep the pearl strands from sliding out.

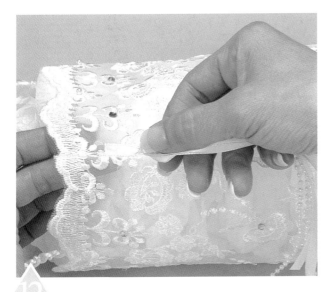

⑫ Attach the Streamers

Glue the ribbon and pearl streamers to the basket seams 1½" (4cm) down from the top of the basket. Randomly slip knot each ribbon and cut the ends diagonally.

CHILD'S PLAY

◆

When you include children in your wedding ceremony, expect anything to happen. But don't worry. If your flower girl should decide to skip down the aisle or dump all of her petals in a pile, your guests will still be enchanted by her beauty, charm and spontaneity.

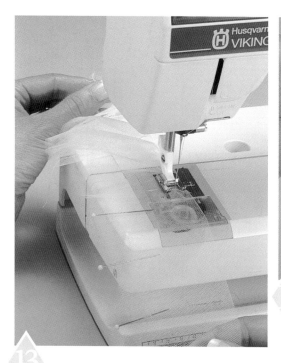

Gather the Tulle

Pull the thread to gather the tulle, and tie all the threads together to form a circle of fabric. Cut the excess thread. Fluff out the tulle and adjust it to form a ball shape.

Baste the Tulle

Fold the tulle lengthwise and press it very lightly to lie flat. Cut a 20" x 6" (51cm x 15cm) piece of tulle and machine baste it along the fold line to make a tulle rose. Sew a ¼" (6mm) seam. Do not cut the thread.

on your wedding day...

If you are having more than one flower girl, ask them to hold hands as they walk down the aisle for mutual support to help ease their nerves.

Add the Tulle Ball

Center the tulle ball on the seam line just over the top of the streamers and glue in place. Fluff the tulle again, hang the basket on a hanger and spray with stiffener. Let the basket dry for one hour. Repeat three times or until the basket is stiff. Let the basket dry each time before spraying again. Don't forget to spray the handle and base.

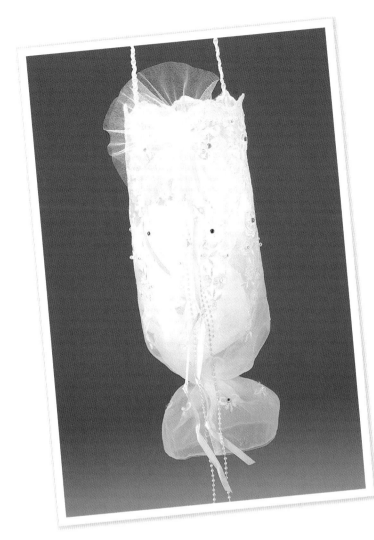

flower girl keepsake

This unique flower girl basket will make a lovely keepsake for your little maid long after your wedding day. To design your own variation, check out the Lace Glossary on page 11 to select from a variety of laces to complement the flower girl's dress. For a variation on the basket handle, try ribbons, a string of beads or pearls, or a small ribbon rose garland. For embellishments, experiment with fresh, silk or dried flowers, ribbon roses, antique jewelry or buttons or pretty bows.

ENTERTAINING CHILDREN

If you are expecting a lot of children at your wedding, think about hiring a sitter or two to help care for the kids at the reception. To entertain the little tykes, reserve kiddie tables at the reception and stock them with goodie bags, candy center-pieces, games and quiet toys. Avoid anything that may stain clothes or little fingers.

UNITY CANDLE

Lighting the unity candle is a visually symbolic part of many wedding ceremonies. Celebrate your union by embellishing plain candles with ribbons and lace to create your own uniquely beautiful unity candle set. A unity candle set usually consists of three candles at the altar. The outer taper candles represent the couple as individuals. The bride and groom take the outer candles, which are lit, and together light the center candle to symbolize the joining of two hearts, two families and their shared commitment to each other in marriage. As a variation, you can also have your parents come forward to light the side tapers to symbolize the two families coming together as one.

materials:

- large pillar candle
- two taper candles
- ¼" (6mm) wide satin ribbon
- ⅛" (3mm) wide satin ribbon
- ½ yd. (46cm) bridal appliqué
- flat-back rhinestones
- fabric glue
- embroidery scissors

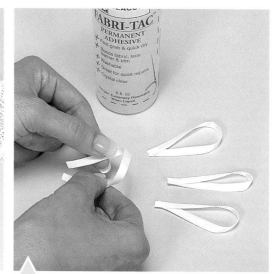

1 Cut Out the Roses

Using embroidery scissors, cut three appliqué roses apart. Cut away two leaves on either side of each rose to allow space for ribbon loops.

2 Make Ribbon Loops

Cut two 5" (13cm) strips of the ¼" (6mm) wide satin ribbon and four 5½" (14cm) strips of the ⅛" (3mm) wide satin ribbon. Make a loop and glue the ends together. Repeat for all strips.

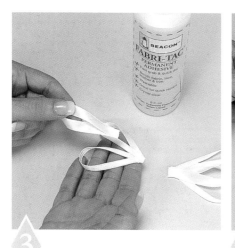

3 Overlap the Loops

Make two stacks of three loops each, with the ¼" (6mm) wide satin ribbon in the middle, and glue them together to form a fan shape.

4 Attach the Ribbon Loops

Glue the fan-shape loops under the rose appliqué in the open space on each side of the rose.

5 Glue the Lace Appliqué

Put fabric glue on the back of the appliqué with loops and let the glue become slightly sticky to the touch. This will take less than one minute. Center the appliqué on the pillar candle. Repeat steps 1–5 for the taper candles. In the center of each rose, glue one rhinestone.

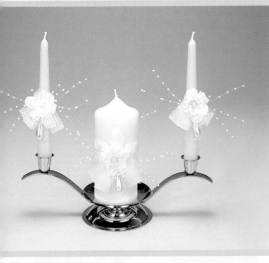

unite by candlelight

Now you have a beautifully embellished unity candle set that will look stunning by candlelight. After you light the center candle, you may blow out the individual flames from the taper candles to symbolize your commitment to each other. Or you can leave all three candles burning throughout the rest of the ceremony to emphasize your individuality within your union. Whether you keep the tapers lit or blow them out is completely up to you, but don't forget to blow out all the candles after the ceremony.

• change the bow

For a different look, these candles have been elegantly embellished with striped satin ribbon, teardrop pearls and silk flowers. When choosing candles for your unity candle set, make sure they have good wicks for easy lighting. Loosen the taper candles from the holders before the ceremony to make them easy to pick up. Leave an extra set of matches nearby in case of an unexpected breeze.

CAKE KNIFE *and* SERVER

Serve your wedding cake in high style with a cake knife and server set embellished with pearls, beads and satin

ribbons. Wedding cakes have become delicious edible art. From trompe l'oeil masterpieces designed to look like

wedding dress lace or elaborate presents to spectacular cakes blooming with fresh or sugarpaste flowers. The

time-honored tradition of the cake-cutting ceremony makes a

great photo opportunity, so your cake knife and server should be

beautifully decorated to complement a gorgeous cake. With so

many decorative ribbons to choose from, you can easily dress

up a plain serving set and give it the finishing touch that adds

a sense of personal style.

materials:

- cake knife and server set
- 2 yd. of $7/8$" (2cm) wide sheer striped ribbon
- 2 yd. (2m) of $7/8$" (2cm) antique ribbon
- $1/8$" (3mm) wide satin ribbon
- sea shell beads
- 5mm pearls
- 24-gauge white wire
- quilt thread
- extra-fine beading needle
- glue gun

• tip •

Use the same technique for creating beaded "paddles" and attach them to shoes, handbags, or even create earrings using an ear clip.

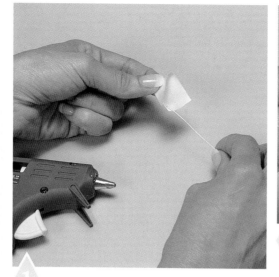

Make a Paddle

Cut two circles each about the size of a quarter (about 1" [3cm] in diameter) from the antique ribbon and cut a 3" (8cm) piece of wire. With the ribbon right side out, hot glue the circles together with the wire in the center. Use only a small amount of glue so you can still sew through the ribbon.

String Pearls and Beads

Thread your beading needle and string the pearls and beads following this pattern: one sea shell bead, one pearl, two sea shell beads, one pearl, one sea shell bead. Do not cut the thread yet! Sew the bead string onto the paddle and tie it off on the back of the paddle. Trim excess thread.

CAKE-CUTTING CEREMONY

◆

As a symbol of fertility and good fortune, the wedding cake is thought to bestow good luck upon all those who take a bite. To cut the cake, the groom places his hand over the bride's and together they cut a piece from the bottom tier of the cake. They feed one another that slice, with the bride taking the first bite. The bride then serves the groom's parents, and the groom serves the bride's parents. The rest of the cake is then cut and served to the guests by the catering staff or preselected volunteers.

Fill the Circle With Beads

Fill the circle with strands of beads following the beading pattern from step 2. Be careful to avoid stitching too close to the ends of the paddle.

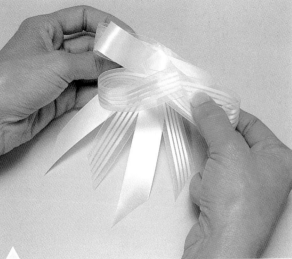

4 Make Streamers

Cut an 11" (28cm) strip of antique ribbon and 10" (25cm) strip of sheer striped ribbon. Fold both ribbons in half and cut them on the fold line so you have four streamers. Overlap the ribbons and hot glue them together in a fan shape. Trim each streamer end with a diagonal cut. Set aside.

Make the Bow

Cut one 10" (25cm) strip of antique ribbon and two 10" (25cm) strips of striped ribbon. Hot glue the ends of each ribbon together to form a bow loop. Stack the three bows on top of each other with the antique ribbon in the center. Hot glue the bows together in the center. Then hot glue the three bows to the center of the streamers.

CAKE PRESENTATION

◆

Display your cake for all to admire. Place regal wedding cakes in your reception area where they'll command the attention of every guest. Drape a round table with a beautiful cloth and line up silver forks for an elegant display. Or dress up a cake table with a cherished family heirloom such as a quilt or lace bedspread.

One place you can create special flower decorations is on the cake table. Floral cake tops are a great way to add color to your wedding cake, and garlands are a lovely floral accent to drape around the cake table. However, be careful not to overdo it. Cake table flowers should only be a complement to an already gorgeous wedding cake and reception decor.

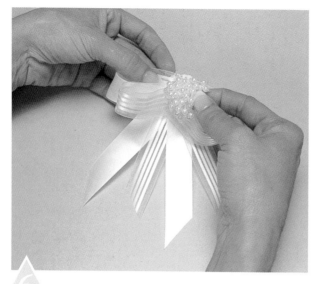

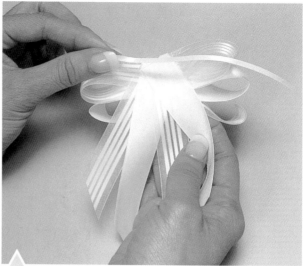

6 Attach Beads

Cut the excess wire and fabric from the beaded circle and hot glue it to the center of the bow.

7 Make the String Tie

Cut a 6½" (17cm) strip of ⅛" (3mm)wide satin ribbon and hot glue it to the back of the bow in the center. This will allow you to tie the bow to the cake knife and server.

DECORATE THE CAKE

◆

Gather pictures of wedding cakes with elements that appeal to you and show them to your baker along with ideas and pictures of your wedding colors, flowers, wedding and reception decorations and your bridal gown. Your cake designer will use all of these to come up with ideas for the cake decoration.

let's eat cake!

Tie on your satin and beaded bow and you have a beautiful cake serving set to cut your wedding cake. Make sure the embellishment on your serving set matches the style of your cake. Add fresh or silk flowers to match your cake decoration or use satin ribbon roses and bows to match an elegant, formal cake.

• change the bow

This variation uses the same bow shown in step 5, but instead of adding beads to the center, I added a smaller bow with loops of pearls. See pages 40–41 of the Flower Girl Headband for instructions on making the bow. Attach the pearl bow to the center of the larger bow with hot glue.

CUTTING CAKE COSTS

◆

Wedding cakes are priced per slice. An average three-tier cake will serve fifty to one hundred guests, while a five-tier cake serves around two hundred. Anything over five tiers is heavy and difficult to maneuver. For larger guest lists, ask your baker to make a smaller decorated cake that's big enough to serve half your guests and serve the remaining slices from sheet cakes kept in the kitchen. This will reduce the expense of an enormous cake, and your guests will never know the difference.

TOASTING FLUTES

You don't need to purchase expensive, engraved toasting flutes. You can doll up plain flutes with anything from a simple white satin ribbon tied to the stems to wrapping them in bridal lace accented with a romantic bow. Initiate the wedding reception toast when the buffet begins or after the guests have been served the first course at a sit-down meal. The best man proposes the first toast to the happiness of the newlyweds. The groom then salutes his bride as well as both sets of parents, and thanks family and friends for sharing his happiness. The bride may toast her new husband, if she wishes, followed by the bride's father and the groom's father. The floor is then open to all who wish to propose short toasts to the couple.

materials:

- two toasting flutes
- 6½" wide 5" long (17cm x 13cm) ruffled lace
- ¼" (6mm) wide satin ribbon
- ⅛" (3mm) wide satin ribbon
- 2½" (6cm) wide sheer wired ribbon
- 8" (20cm) 3mm pearl strand
- 8" (20cm) 3mm iridescent pearl strand
- two beaded appliqués
- fabric glue
- white 40 wt. thread
- hand-sewing needle

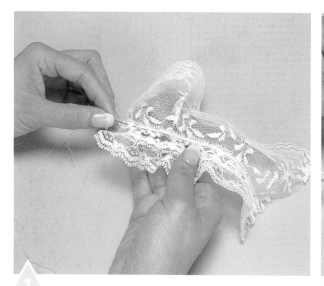

1 Stitch the Ruffle

Hand sew a running stitch about 3" (8cm) from the bottom of the lace ruffle. Do not cut the thread.

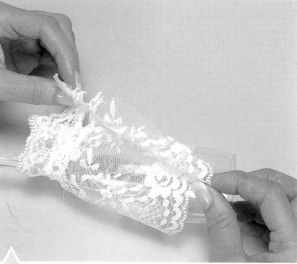

2 Glue the Lace to the Flute

Starting at 2" (5cm) from the top of the flute, glue the lace to the glass by going around the flute and overlapping the lace to match the scallop pattern.

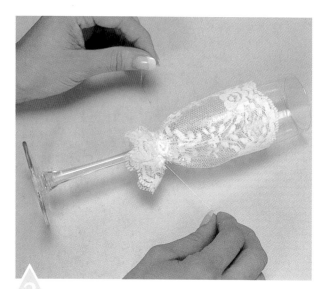

3 Gather the Lace

Pull both ends of the thread like a drawstring to gather the lace together at the glass stem. Wrap the thread two times around the stem to secure, tie the thread and cut any excess.

4 Cover the Thread

Cut one 4"(10cm) strand of $\frac{1}{8}$" (3mm) wide satin ribbon and wrap it around the gathered lace at the top of the glass stem to cover the thread.

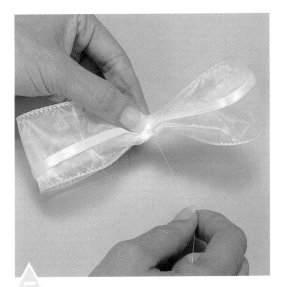

5 Create the Bow

Cut both the sheer wired ribbon and $\frac{1}{4}$" (6mm) wide satin ribbon to 13" (33cm) each. Glue the satin ribbon down the center of the wired ribbon. Hold one end of the double ribbon between your thumb and index finger and make a loop on each side of your thumb. Gather the bow in the center by wrapping it tightly with thread. Cut any excess thread.

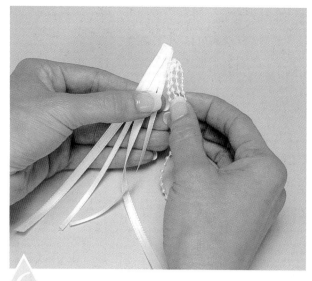

6 Create the Streamers

Cut two 8" (20cm) strands of ⅛" (3mm) wide satin ribbon. Fold each one in half to make a V shape. Glue them together at the fold. If you are using spools of pearl stands, cut an 8" (20cm) strand of iridescent pearls and plain pearls. Fold them into a V shape and glue them on top of the ribbon streamers. Glue the pearls to the ribbon, then glue the streamers to the middle of the flute to hide the lace seam.

7 Add the Bow

Center the bow on top of the streamers and glue it down. Allow the glue to dry. Glue the beaded appliqué to the center of the bow. Randomly tie slipknots along the streamers. Cut the ends of the ribbon with a diagonal cut.

·tip·

When gluing embellishments to the flutes, put the glue on the lace or ribbons, not the glass, to avoid glue splotches on the glass. Put your embellishments on the seam of the lace to hide it for a more finished look.

toast **to** love

There are so many ways to dress up plain toasting flutes. Just use your imagination! Using decorative ribbon, tie a simple bow at the top of the stem and hot glue small silk or fresh flowers such as stephanotis or sweetheart roses to the center. Add embellishments such as tiny gold rings, feathers or crystals. Just remember to make sure any embellishments are secured to the glass to hold up to being handled and avoid putting anything too close to the rim of the glass that may get in the way of drinking.

· tip ·

Decorate your toasting flutes similarly to the cake knife and server since they will be photographed together on the cake table. See the Cake Knife & Server on page 88 for embellishment ideas.

SECTION 4

WEDDING
KEEPSAKES

No matter how well planned your wedding is, you can't stop time, even on your wedding day. In the midst of all the excitement, it just isn't possible to memorize every detail and capture every pose. Keepsakes are a wonderful and creative way to capture and cherish those precious memories that might otherwise fade.

Once you create your keepsakes, you will want to make sure they last. This section discusses how to preserve your keepsakes, with special attention paid to your wedding gown, flowers, photographs and other memorabilia. Enable your memories to last more than a lifetime. Get tips on cleaning and storing your wedding gown, air-drying or freeze-drying your flowers and organizing and preserving your wedding photos.

KEEPSAKE BOX · MEMORY QUILT

KEEPSAKE BOX

Store all of your cherished wedding memorabilia in this satin-covered keepsake box. With its gently padded

interior you can place delicate items such as glass or sterling silver keepsakes inside for safekeeping. Satin

ribbon straps along the interior sides and bottom of the box are perfect for holding love letters and cards or

treasured photos. To transform a simple cardboard box into an

elegant keepsake box, personalize it with a fabric reminiscent

of your wedding dress and embellish it with ribbon-wrapped

hearts, silk or ribbon flowers or a simple yet elegant bow.

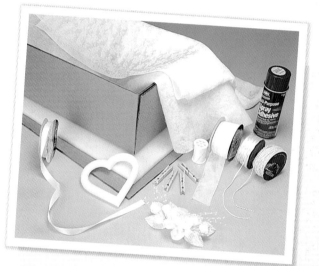

materials:

- 12" wide x 22$\frac{1}{2}$" long x 7" deep (30cm x 57cm x 18cm) cardboard box with lid

- two 12" x 22$\frac{1}{2}$" (30cm x 57cm) cardboard sheets

- 5 yd. (5m) Dominique satin (any bridal satin will work)

- 3 yd. (3m) lightweight quilt batting

- 3 yd. (3m) of $\frac{1}{2}$" (1cm) wide foam

- 12 yd. (11m) of 2" (5cm) wide sheer wired ribbon

- 3 yd. (3m) of 1" (3cm) wide satin ribbon

- 3 yd. (3m) 3mm pearl strand

- 3 yd. (3m) rattail cording

- 11" (28cm) pearl spray

- bridal flower spray

- two 6" (15cm) plastic foam hearts

- spray adhesive

- masking tape

- eight to ten clothespins

- ruler

- white 40 wt. thread

- hand-sewing needle

- glue gun

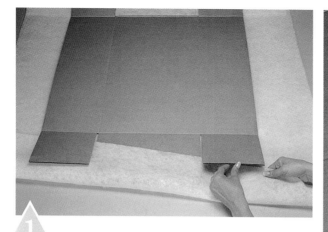

1

Center the Box

Cut the satin fabric and quilt batting to $50\frac{1}{2}$" x 41" (128cm x 104cm). Lay the satin face down and apply spray adhesive to the wrong side of the fabric. Lay the batting on top of the fabric, keeping the batting as smooth as you can so it adheres flat to the fabric. Open the bottom of the box so it lies flat and center it on top of the batting. On each end of the box, fold the fabric and batting over the seam lines of the box. Put all four box ends on top of the fabric to center the box. Once the box is centered, reopen the fabric to lie flat. (Do not move the box from its position.)

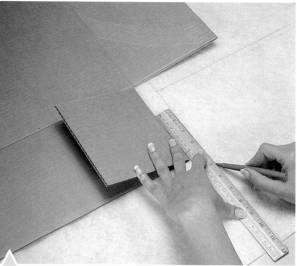

2

Mark the Cutting Line

Fold up the box corner, place a ruler next to the seam line and draw a 1" (3cm) wide line to the edge of the fabric. Lay the ruler next to the side flap and draw a 1" (3cm) wide line to the end of the fabric. Repeat these measurements for the remaining three corners of the box.

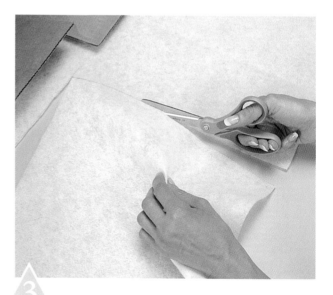

3

Cut Out Squares

Cutting both the batting and fabric as one piece, cut out a square from the corner of the fabric following your line measurements. Repeat for each corner.

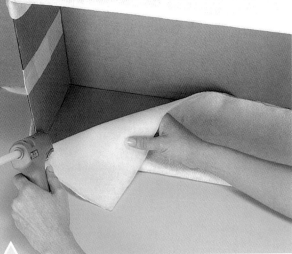

Tape the Box Corners

Fold up the long sides of the box to join the box corners and secure with masking tape.

Glue Fabric to the Box

Bring the fabric and batting over the side of the long side of the box and hot glue them to the inside wall. Repeat for the opposite side of the box. Use clothespins to hold the fabric and batting in place until they are secure.

NOTE: *The fabric should come down the inside wall and overlap 1" (3cm) onto the bottom of the box.*

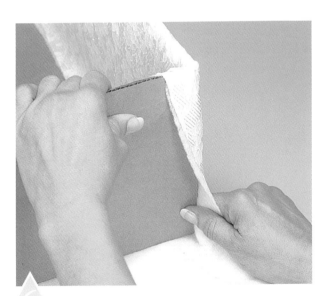

Glue Fabric to the Side Corners

Start at the top of the outside corner of the box. Fold the fabric over onto the box and hot glue it in place, keeping the fabric and batting smooth. Repeat for all corners.

on your wedding day...

In addition to saving keepsakes from your wedding day, consider saving items from your engagement and first year of marriage, too.

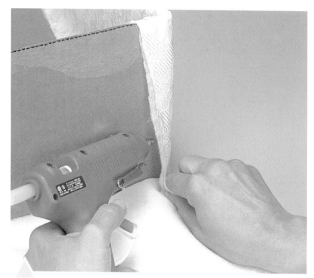

Glue Fabric to the Bottom Corners

Make a small cut in the fabric at the bottom corner. This will allow the fabric to lie flat. Pull the small flap inward along the side of the box and hot glue in place. Hold the flap in place until glue is dry. Repeat for the other corners.

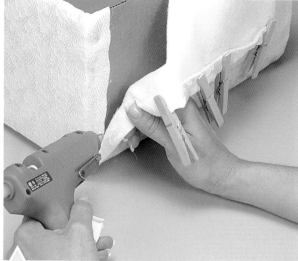

Glue Fabric to the Outside Corners

Fold the fabric back onto itself by 1" (3cm) and hot glue it down to the end of the fabric. Use clothespins to hold it in place until it is dry. Begin to pull up the fabric at the outside corner, and hot glue it along the edge of the box up to the top corner while keeping the fabric very smooth.

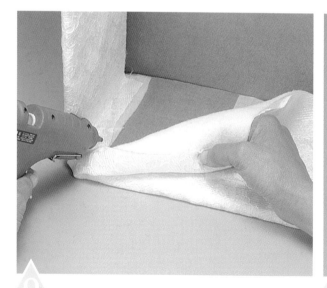

Glue Fabric to the Inside Corners

Turn the box on its side. Begin pulling the fabric over to the inside wall of the box, and glue it to the corner seam line. Hold it in place until the glue is dry. Repeat for the other sides. Turn the box upright and continue to hot glue the fabric inside the bottom of the box. Allow the glue to dry.

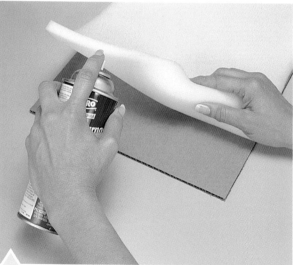

Attach the Foam to the Cardboard Sheet

Cut the foam and cardboard sheet $\frac{1}{2}$" (1cm) smaller than the bottom of the box. Lay the cardboard flat and apply the spray adhesive. Center the foam on the top of the cardboard.

NOTE: *Use an old sheet or newspaper to protect your table surface from the spray adhesive.*

Attach Fabric to the Cardboard Sheet

Cut the fabric and batting to 15" x 25" (38cm x 64cm). Lay the fabric face side down. Apply spray adhesive to the fabric and lay the batting on top. Center the cardboard foam side down on top of the fabric. Fold the fabric over onto the back of cardboard and secure with masking tape.

Secure the Corners

Fold down the right end of the fabric using a small amount of hot glue to hold it in place. Fold the fabric over to the left and hot glue in place. Hold until glue is dry. Repeat for all corners.

HONEYMOON KEEPSAKES

When you are on your honeymoon, pick up small items that can later be saved in your keepsake box. Here are few ideas to get you started:

- brochures
- coasters
- foreign currency
- maps
- matches
- photos
- playbills
- postcards
- pressed leaves and flowers
- receipts
- shells, sand and rocks
- ticket stubs

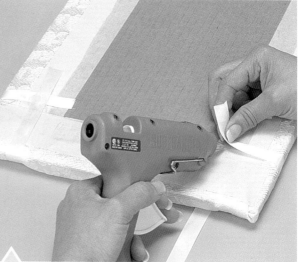

Add Ribbon Straps

Cut two 30" (76cm) and two 19" (48cm) strands of satin ribbon. Lay the two 30" (76cm) ribbons on top of the fabric-covered cardboard lengthwise, one 3" (8cm) from the top edge and the other 3" (8cm) from the bottom edge. Pin them in place. Repeat this with the two 19" (48cm) ribbons on the short ends of the fabric-covered cardboard. Pin the ribbons in place running in opposite directions. Hand stitch the ribbons at each intersection. Do not remove the pins yet.

Secure the Ribbon Ends

On the back of the fabric-covered cardboard, secure each ribbon end with hot glue and remove the pins. Repeat steps 1–14 to cover the lid of the box.

· tip ·

Instead of hot glue, you can hand stitch the bows to each intersection if you wish.

Attach the Bows

Cut twelve 13" (33cm) satin ribbons and tie each ribbon in a shoestring bow. Hot glue a bow to each ribbon intersection on the fabric-covered cardboard sheets (for a total of eight bows). Position each bow with the ends toward the center. Clip the ribbon ends diagonally. Hold onto the remaining four bows for step 17.

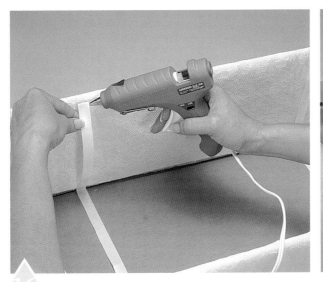

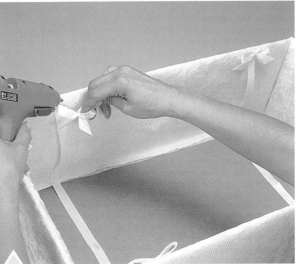

16 Add Ribbon Straps

Cut two 30" (76cm) satin ribbons. Fold each ribbon end under 1" (3cm) and hot glue each end to the top edge of the box 3" (8cm) in from the corner on the long side of the box. Pull the ribbons loosely down the inside wall and glue them to the bottom seam of the box.

17 Attach Bows to the Straps

Hot glue (or stitch) a bow to the top edge of each strap, and place the finished fabric-covered cardboard sheets in the top and bottom of the box. Secure the fabric-covered cardboard sheets with hot glue.

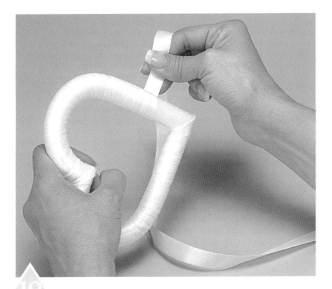

on your wedding day...

Take both black-and-white and color photographs of your special wedding moments. Color photos last for around fifty years while black and white photos last up to one hundred years.

18 Wrap the Hearts

Hot glue one end of the satin ribbon to the bottom of the heart and wrap the entire heart. Overlap the ribbon as you wrap. Secure the end of the ribbon with hot glue. Repeat for the other heart.

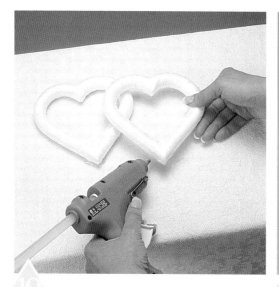

19 Attach the Hearts

Center the two hearts on the lid of the box and hot glue them in place, one at a time. Hold each heart until the glue is dry.

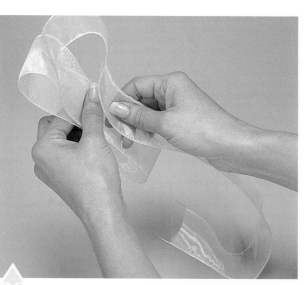

20 Make a Sheer Wire Bow

Cut a 65" (2m) piece of sheer wired ribbon. Leaving one ribbon end free, hold the ribbon between your thumb and index finger. Form a loop on each side of your thumb. Make four loops on each side. Secure the loops with a 4" (10cm) satin ribbon by wrapping the ribbon around the loops in the center and tie it tightly. Cut the excess ribbon.

21 Add Streamers

Cut four 20" (51cm) strands of pearls and four 20" (51cm) lengths of cording. Fold all the pearl strands and cording in half (as one unit) to form a loop. Cut a 4" (10cm) satin ribbon. Thread one end of the ribbon through the loop and tie it tightly. This will give you a tab to hot glue to the box.

22 Add the Bow and Flower

Put a small amount of hot glue on the ribbon tab to secure the streamers to the box between the two hearts on the lid. Tie a knot at the end of each cording streamer. Center the flower spray and pearl spray just under the two hearts over the streamers and hot glue them in place. Hold them in place until the glue is dry.

• add a bow!

For this variation, the same

cardboard box was covered in

white rose taffeta instead of

satin, and it's embellished with

an elaborate bow. Screw small

drawer pulls into the bottom of

the box for feet so you can protect

the fabric on the bottom of the

box. See the Bridal Fabric Guide

on page 11 for a list of fabrics to

choose from to create your own

custom keepsake box.

fill your box with wedding treasures!

To protect and preserve your wedding memorabilia, line your box with acid-free tissue paper. As a variation to this box design, instead of covering your box with fabric, you can also use handmade paper, decorative wallpaper or heavy gift wrap. If you choose to use a plain wooden box instead of cardboard, try painting it white and stenciling designs on the sides and lid.

MEMORY QUILT

Keep the memories of your wedding day alive with this beautiful wedding quilt that commemorates the names of your closest family and friends who attended your wedding celebration. When guests arrive at the reception, ask them to sign a fabric square with permanent fabric pen. After the wedding, use these signed squares to create a stunning keepsake quilt that will quickly become a cherished heirloom. Store your memory quilt in your keepsake box (see page 102) or add hanging tabs and a decorative rod and display it on a wall.

· tip ·

Tape three or four thin strips of very fine sandpaper across the bottom of your quilter's ruler using double-sided tape. This will keep your ruler from slipping while you are cutting fabric.

materials:

- 3 yd. (3m) white 100% cotton muslin
- 6 yd. (5m) white-on-white patterned 100% cotton
- 3 yd. (3m) off-white 100% cotton
- 3 yd. (3m) lightweight quilt batting
- ¼" (6mm) wide chiffon ribbon
- 2" (5cm) wide wired chiffon ribbon
- 15 yd. (14m) of ½" (1cm) wide rose vine appliqué braid
- thirty-two 1" (3cm) drop pearls
- three pearl sprays
- 16-gauge clear vinyl plastic (½" [1cm] bigger on all sides than your wedding invitation)

- wedding invitation
- 3 yd. (3m) double-sided transfer web paper
- quilter's ruler
- masking tape
- heart template (SEE PAGE 116)
- permanent fabric pen
- glue stick
- white and yellow 40 wt. thread
- 4mm quilter's pins
- #7 quilter's needle
- rotary cutter and mat
- glue gun

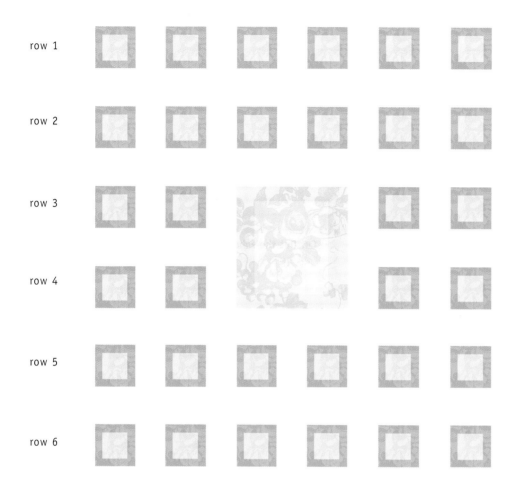

row 1

row 2

row 3

row 4

row 5

row 6

Before sewing your Memory Quilt, follow these guidelines: Lay out all of the cut pieces according to the diagram. This will let you know if a piece is missing and simplify your piecing row by row. As you sew each section, put it back in position to make piecing easier. Use a $\frac{1}{4}$" (6mm) seam allowance when sewing the quilt. Prewash all fabric, and press first for easier cutting.

CUTTING DIRECTIONS

• • •

FABRIC	CUTTING QUANTITY	SIZE TO CUT
White patterned cotton	32 background squares	6" x 6" (15cm x 15cm)
Muslin	32 name squares	5" x 5" (13cm x 13cm)
White patterned cotton	1 center square	13½" x 13½" (34cm x 34cm)
Clear vinyl plastic	1 center plastic sleeve	8½" x 6" (22cm x 15cm)
Quilt batting	1 quilt batting	50" x 52" (127cm x 132cm)
White patterned cotton	1 quilt back	50" x 52" (127cm x 132cm)
Off-white cotton	24 bar straps	6" x 2" (15cm x 5cm)
	2 interior bar straps	13½" x 2" (34cm x 5cm)
	2 outside borders	52" x 2" (132cm x 5cm)
	2 top/bottom borders	46" x 2" (117cm x 5cm)
	4 interior sashes	46" x 2" (117cm x 5cm)
	2 short sashes	14" x 2" (36cm x 5cm)

Cut the Fabric Edges

Fold the fabric in half lengthwise with the right sides together. The fold line should follow along the grain of the fabric. Lay the fabric on the cutting mat with the fold line along a grid line. Place the quilter's ruler on the fabric close to the raw edge at a 90° angle to the fold. Use your rotary cutter to trim along the edge of the ruler. Keeping a steady pressure, hold the ruler firmly to keep the fabric from moving. Once the rotary cutter gets past your hand, leave the rotary blade in position and reposition your hand. Hold firmly and continue cutting. Make sure the fabric and ruler do not shift position.

Cut Out the Fabric Squares

Place the ruler on the fabric, aligning the trimmed edge with the appropriate measurement on the ruler. Hold the ruler firmly and cut as in step 1. After cutting several strips, check the fabric to make sure all the fabric pieces are "on grain", as in step 1. Follow the cutting directions on page 114.

Piece the Quilt Together

Instead of cutting each piece of the quilt individually, stack several layers of fabric and cut them into crosswise strips. Once you have cut out all the fabric pieces according to the cutting directions on page 114, lay out all the fabric pieces according to the Quilt Layout Diagram. This will show you if something is missing from your quilt pattern.

BASIC CUTTING AND PIECING TECHNIQUES

◆

Accuracy in cutting is critical to successfully piecing the quilt. A small error can multiply itself resulting in a quilt that doesn't fit together. The cutting techniques on this page will not only save you time but also keep your cuts more accurate. Before you start cutting, determine the grain line of the fabric by folding the fabric in half and holding it by the rough edges.

HEART TEMPLATE
enlarge 125%

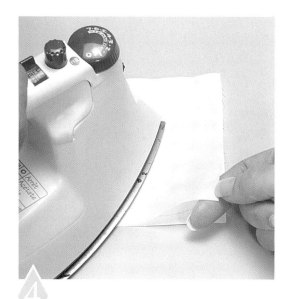

4 **Iron on the Transfer Web**

Iron the transfer web to the wrong side of all thirty-two white muslin squares following the directions on the transfer web package.

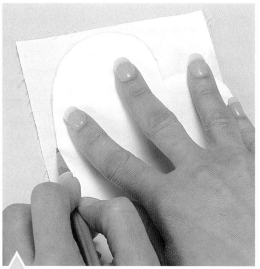

5 **Trace the Heart**

Use the heart template to trace a heart on the transfer web paper on the back of the muslin squares, and cut out all thirty-two hearts.

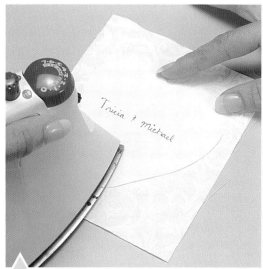

6 **Write Names on the Hearts**

Use the fabric pen to write names on the right side of the fabric in the center of each heart (or have the guests sign the hearts themselves at the wedding reception to save you a step). Score the transfer web paper backing with a pin and remove all the paper from the hearts.

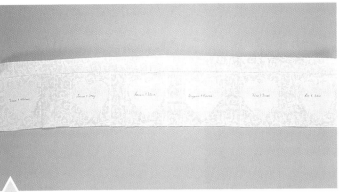

Iron Hearts to the Fabric

Center the hearts on each background fabric square and press into place. *(This photo shows rows 1 and 2.)*

Sew the Squares and Bar Straps Together

Sewing one square at a time, with the right sides of fabric together, sew each background square to a 6" x 2" (15cm x 5cm) bar strap and return to its proper position. Now sew the opposite side of the background square and a bar strap together. Continue until you complete row 1. Press all seams flat. Repeat this step for rows 2, 3a, 3b, 4a, 4b, 5 and 6 on the quilt-piecing diagram below. *(This photo shows row 1 completed with the top border.)*

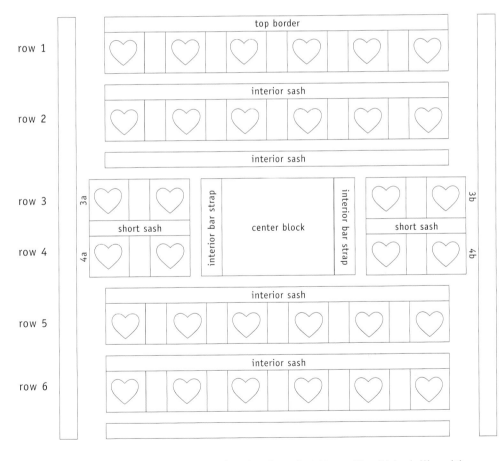

Add the Borders

With the right sides of the fabric together, sew the top border to row 1, and the interior sashes to rows 2, 5 and 6. Return the rows to their proper layout position as you sew.

With the right sides of the fabric together sew row 3a to a short sash and then sew this unit to row 4a. Repeat for rows 3b and 4b. Sew the two interior bar straps to the center block, one on each side. Now sew the three middle blocks together to make one unit and sew the center interior sash to the top. Return all the pieces to their layout position.

• Quilt diagram for steps 8 and 9 showing what the quilt will look like with all the heart blocks sewn to all the interior bar straps, interior sashes and short sashes.

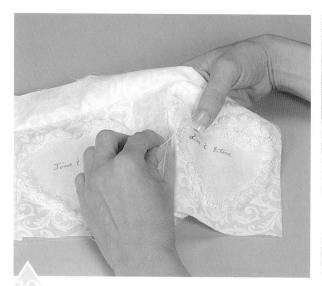 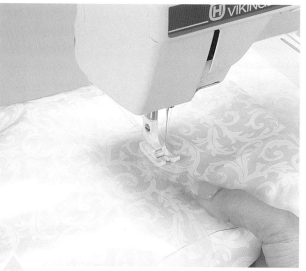

Add the Braid to the Hearts

Pin the rose vine appliqué braid to each heart. Overlap the braid at the top of each heart and trim any excess braid. Hand stitch the braid in place around each heart.

Sew the Plastic Pocket

Center the clear vinyl plastic on the center square and tape it in place with masking tape (do not use pins!). Sew $\frac{1}{4}$" (6mm) seam allowance. As you sew the plastic, remove the tape when you come to it to avoid getting tape adhesive on the needle.

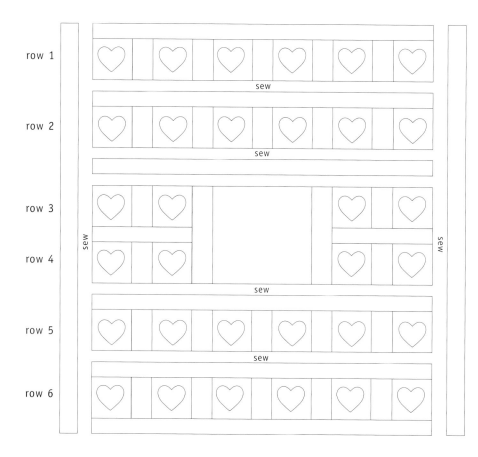

row 1

sew

row 2

sew

row 3

row 4

sew

row 5

sew

row 6

sew

sew

Sew the Rows Together

Following the diagram on the left, sew each row together to form the quilt top and press.

• Quilt diagram for step 12

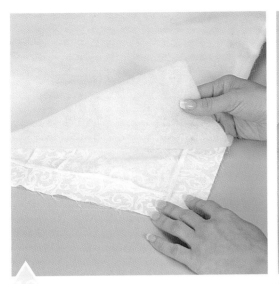

Add the Batting

With the quilt face side down on the table, tape all the corners down to keep the quilt from moving around. Lay the batting on top of the quilt, pin it to the quilt, then remove the tape and turn the quilt over.

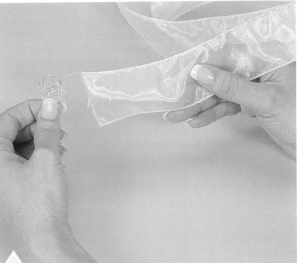

Pull Out the Wire

Pull the wire free from one side of the 15 yd. (14m) wired chiffon ribbon. When pulling the wire out of the ribbon, wrap the wire into a ball as you pull it out. This will keep the wire under control.

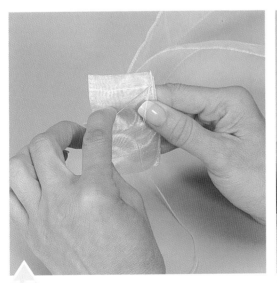

Sew the Ribbon Ends

Hand stitch the ends of the ribbon together to secure. Cut and tie the thread, making sure the ribbon isn't twisted.

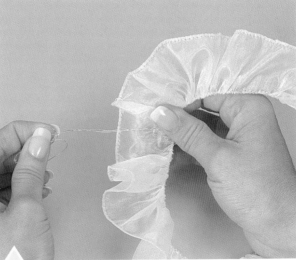

Form a Ruffle

Pull the wire ends of the chiffon ribbon together and twist. As the ribbon begins to gather, pin the ruffle to the front perimeter of the quilt. Continue to pull the wire, pivoting at the corners and pinning as you go along the ruffle. Adjust the gathers to fit the quilt front. Do not cut the wire.

NOTE: *The wire side of the ruffle should be next to the edge of the quilt.*

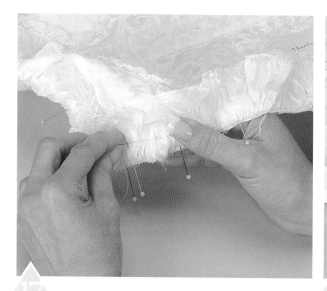

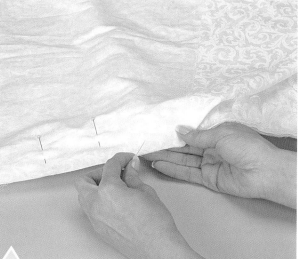

Baste the Ruffle

Hand baste the ribbon ruffle to the quilt and batting $\frac{1}{2}$" (1cm) from the raw edge. Remove all pins.

Add the Quilt Back

Pin the quilt back to the quilt front over the ruffle with the right sides of the fabric together. Machine stitch around the quilt leaving a 10" (25cm) opening for turning. Cut the corners diagonally and trim to a $\frac{1}{8}$" (3mm) seam allowance. Untwist the wire ends and remove the rest of the wire from the quilt. Turn the quilt right side out and slip stitch the opening to close.

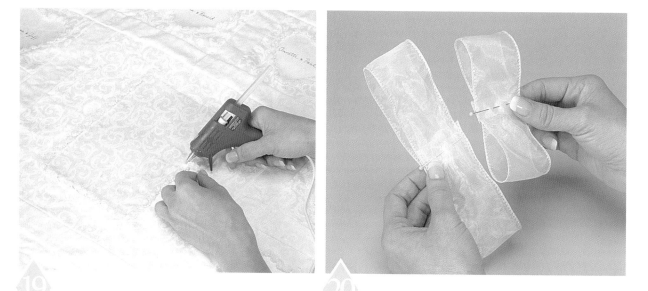

Add the Braid to the Pocket

Hot glue the rose vine appliqué braid around the clear plastic pocket, leaving the top free. Cut any excess braid and hot glue the ends down.

Make the Bow

Cut two pieces of 2" (5cm) wide wired chiffon ribbon to 11$\frac{1}{2}$" (29cm) and 17$\frac{1}{2}$" (44cm) and mark the center of both ribbons. To make the bow, overlap the ribbon $\frac{1}{4}$" (6mm) at the center and pin in place.

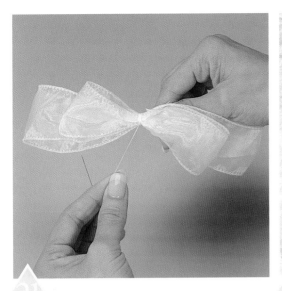

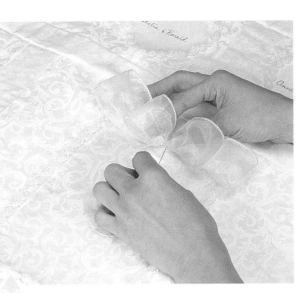

21 **Sew the Bow Together**

Lay the small bow on top of the large bow, matching the centers, and hand baste both together. Pull the thread to allow the bow to gather in the center, and wrap the thread tightly around the center of the bow a few times. To secure the bow, cut the thread and tie the ends in a knot.

22 **Attach the Bow**

Above the clear plastic pocket, center the bow and hand stitch into place.

 tip

Avoid wearing color nail polish when working with white fabric to keep it from getting stained.

23 **Add the Pearl Spray**

On each side of the bow, hot glue two pearl sprays between the small and large loops of the bow. Insert your wedding invitation into the plastic pocket. Hot glue one pearl spray to the center of the bow just under the gather.

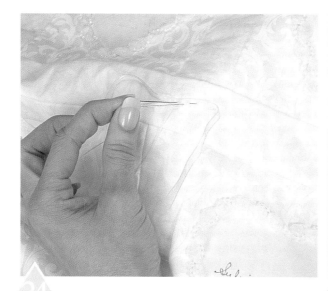

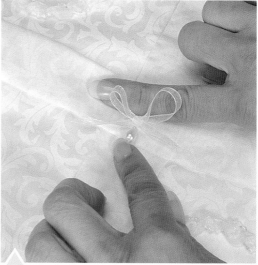

Attach the Ribbon

Cut a 9" (23cm) length of ¼" (6mm) wide chiffon ribbon and mark the center. Hand stitch the ribbon in the center through all three layers of the quilt at every intersection, and tie a triple knot. Tie a shoestring bow with each ribbon.

Add a Drop Pearl

Hot glue a drop pearl to the center of each bow.

create an heirloom

This one-of-a-kind quilt will quickly become your most cherished keepsake. As a variation, showcase your wedding photo in the center pocket instead of your invitation. If you had your dress designed, create the quilt with leftover bridal fabric from your dress. For proper storage in a keepsake box, pack your quilt with acid-free tissue paper.

After your big day is over, you will want to relive your wedding memories again and again. Preserve keepsake items from your wedding such as your gown, bouquet, photos, invitation, honeymoon postcards, and more and save these treasured mementos for many years to come. If stored properly they will become cherished heirlooms to pass down to your own children long after your wedding day is over.

Preserving Your Wedding Gown

No other garment has more value to you than your wedding gown. Whether you choose to keep it for yourself as a cherished memento or you save it for your daughter to wear on her wedding day, your gown deserves to be preserved. Make sure it is properly cleaned and stored so it will remain a beautiful treasured keepsake.

CLEANING AND STORAGE • Food, drink and makeup stains are lethal to a wedding dress,

and body oils will turn the fabric yellow. Find a dry cleaner that offers wedding gown cleaning services and send your gown to be cleaned within one to six months after the wedding. Ask to see the dress before it is packed away for storage to make sure all visible stains have been removed.

Wedding gowns should be packed with acid-free tissue in between the folds of the dress and in the bodice to prevent wrinkles and placed in a storage box to protect it from light, insects and acid. Avoid boxes with cellophane windows that allow light to hit the dress. Light can discolor fabric over time. All the shoulder pads, perspiration shields and anything else made of foam should be removed from the gown. Foam deteriorates and breaks down, which may damage the surrounding material. Avoid packing your gown with plastic or metal buttons, pins or buckles. And you should never put mothballs or crystals near your gown. The chemicals used in all of these can ruin fabric over time.

Never hang your wedding gown for long-term storage. Also, never seal the storage box completely. Your gown needs proper air circulation or the fabric and lace will dry out and begin to deteriorate. Avoid extreme temperatures like cold basements or hot attics. Major shifts in temperature, moisture or direct sunlight can damage your gown. Once your gown is cleaned and boxed, store it in a closet or under a bed.

You can have your dress professionally packed away or you can do it yourself after it has been dry-cleaned. To do it yourself, get a large box or cedar chest, acid-free tissue paper and a cotton liner. Never use brown or plastic boxes because they contain materials that are harmful to delicate fabric. Carefully arrange the bodice and skirt to avoid wrinkles and crumple tissue paper in the major folds to prevent big creases.

Don't be afraid to take your gown out of the box from time to time. It's a good idea to check it to make sure it is holding up in storage and still looks as beautiful as the day you wore it. Wear white cotton gloves to prevent any oils from your hands from staining the dress.

Preserving Wedding Flowers

There are many ways to preserve the flowers from your bouquet, ceremony or reception arrangements. Flowers can be air-dried, dried in silica gel or preserved through freeze-drying. Air-dried and freeze-dried flowers may be dried with the stems attached, while flowers dried in silica gel are dried without the stems.

AIR-DRYING • While there are several methods of air-drying flowers, hanging them upside down in a dark, dry and well-ventilated space will dry most varieties. When dry, the flowers will be smaller than their original size, color may be lost and the petals and leaves will have a wrinkled appearance. Most flowers dry within five days to two weeks.

SILICA GEL • Available in most craft stores, silica gel is a powder that dries flower heads to a nearly fresh appearance within several days. It absorbs moisture from the flowers while supporting their natural shape. Silica gel can also be reused several times. Simply place the flower heads face up in a container partially filled with the silica gel powder, preferably an airtight container that is shallow and large in diameter. Gently sprinkle silica gel between the flower petals, then cover the flowers completely with the powder. Tightly cover the container with a lid and allow the flowers to dry for two to seven days. The process must be checked daily so the flowers do not overdry and become brittle. Finally, remove the dried flowers with a slotted spoon, gently lifting them from the

powder. Remove the excess silica gel from the flower petals with a soft brush. These flowers can now be used for arranging but will need to have wire stems added for support.

FREEZE-DRYING • Freeze-drying is an advanced drying process that can preserve a flower almost indefinitely. Freeze-dried flowers keep their shape and color, can be used easily in arrangements and the stem never has to be cut from the flower head. To have your flowers freeze-dried, take them to a professional florist who specializes in this process.

Freeze-drying has become known as a near-perfect method of flower preservation. The freeze-drier removes the water from the flower at subzero temperatures through a vacuum. The moisture is collected in a condensation chamber and defrosted throughout the preservation time. The flowers are then warmed to room temperature. The process takes ten to fifteen days and allows the flowers to hold their natural size and shape as well as their vibrant color. Love may be eternal, but most wedding bouquets die quickly. The freeze-drying process can keep your wedding bouquet looking as beautiful as the day you carried it down the aisle.

Preserving Memorabilia

After your wedding you will have a wealth of special photos and a variety of memorabilia from matchbooks to invitations. Store them in a keepsake box, wedding album or wedding scrapbook. When working with keepsake books, use acid- and lignin-free albums and paper products, photo-safe adhesives, PVC-free plastics and pigment inks to properly preserve your photos and keepsakes.

As you begin to organize your wedding photos, write down memories that the photos inspire. Consider enlarging your favorite photos. Add handwritten journaling pages to your album or scrapbook for a personal touch. Customize your keepsake book with rubber stamps, stickers, photo corners, punches, and decorative scrapbook papers. Don't forget to save memorabilia from your engagement, bridal shower, bachelorette party and honeymoon.

KEEPSAKE IDEAS

In addition to photographs, here's a starter list of possible items to save as keepsakes from your engagement to your wedding. For honeymoon keepsake ideas, see page 107.

- copy of gift registry
- garter
- guest favors
- guest list
- guest signatures
- handwritten vows

- love letters
- marriage license
- matchbooks
- menu card
- napkins
- pressed flowers

- receipts
- sheet music
- shower invitation
- table confetti
- thank-you card
- wedding invitation

RESOURCE DIRECTORY

Resources

COATS & CLARK, INC.
30 Patewood Drive, Ste #351
Greenville, SC 29615
864-281-5521
www.coatsandclark.com

• *sewing and embroidery threads*

FISKARS, INC.
305 84th Ave. South
Wausau, WI 54401
715-842-2091
www.fiskars.com

• *fabric scissors*

HOME-SEW
P.O. Box 4099
Bethlehem, PA 18018
800-344-4739

• *sewing and crafting supplies*

MOUNTAIN MIST
100 Williams Street
Cincinnati, OH 45215
800-345-7150
mountain.mist@stearnstextiles.com
www.stearnstextiles.com

• *quilting supplies and techniques*

C.M. OFFRAY & SON INC.
360 Route 24
Chester, NJ 07930
908-879-4700
www.offray.com

• *decorative ribbons and trims*

THEM O WEB
770 Glenn Ave.
Wheeling, IL 60090
www.themoweb.com

• *fusible web*

WRIGHTS
85 South Street
P.O. Box 398
West Warren, MA 01092-0398
www.wrights.com

• *decorative ribbons*

WEDDING WEB SITES

◆

For general information about wedding planning, etiquette, fashions and trends, check out these helpful web sites:

www.blisswedding.com

www.bridalguide.com

www.bridesofcolor.com

www.TheKnot.com

www.ModernBride.com

www.usabride.com

www.weddingbells.com

Bibliography

Blum, Marcy and Laura Fisher Kaiser. *Weddings for Dummies™*. Foster City, CA: IDG Books Worldwide, 1997.

Memory Makers. *Wedding Idea Book*. Denver, CO: Satellite Press, 2000.

Norden, Mary. *Wedding Details*. New York, NY: Ryland Peters & Small/HarperCollins, 2000.

Roney, Carley. *The Knot's Complete Guide to Weddings in the Real World*. New York, NY: Broadway Books, 1998.

Warner, Diane. *Beautiful Wedding Decorations & Gifts on a Small Budget*. Cincinnati, OH: Betterway Books, 1995.

INDEX

PERSONALIZE your wedding with *Elegant*

handmade keepsakes and decorations!

Create your very own floral arrangements for priceless wedding memories with a personal touch. Terry Rye will teach you step by step how to design more than 20 stunning designs. You'll find something for every part of the wedding—from the bride's bouquet and boutonnieres to pew decorations, table centerpieces and wedding cake toppers.

ISBN 1-55870-560-0, paperback, 128 pages, #70488-K

Want to plan a stunning wedding on a budget you can afford? This book shows you how to do so without sacrificing quality or elegance. It also provides information on the latest wedding trends (with advice for being fashionable at a low price), creative new cost-cutting ideas and dozens of useful tips that will help save time and money!

ISBN 1-55870-646-1, paperback, 192 pages, #70594-K

Make your wedding elegant and unforgettable with these beautiful keepsake ideas. From the bridal veil to the guest book, this book provides 18 step-by-step projects that are fun, affordable and surprisingly easy to make. Best of all, each project is made from non-perishable materials, so everything can be finished well in advance of the big day.

ISBN 1-55870-559-7, paperback, 128 pages, #70487-K

This unique guide combines dazzling layout ideas with easy-to-follow instructions for creating a gorgeous wedding scrapbook album. You'll find layouts for every event, including the engagement, shower, wedding ceremony, reception, honeymoon and more. Every aspect of the scrapbooking process is covered, from organizing photos and selecting an album to choosing a visual theme and writing journal entries.

ISBN 1-89212-708-3, paperback, 128 pages, #31788-K

These titles are available from your local art & craft retailer, bookseller, online supplier or by calling 1-800-448-0915.